TV-am

Official Celebration of the

ROYAL WEDDING

Gordon Honeycombe

Weidenfeld and Nicolson
London

ACKNOWLEDGEMENTS

I am indebted to all the journalists, reporters, correspondents, authors and other writers who have already written about the people and events in this book. My thanks to them, and to the Press Office at Buckingham Palace. My special thanks for their specialised information and help to Dickie Arbiter, Sara Barrett, John Boyd, Richard Broome, Adrian Brown, Glynn Christian, Nigel Dempster, David Foster, Martin Frizell, Cathy Galvin, Wendy Keith, Keith Magloire, Charlotte McGowan, Hugh Montgomery-Massingberd, Hugh Poole-Warren, Bryan Rostron, Ann Smit, Phil Tomkinson, Peter Tory, and Jane Vallance. My particular gratitude to Martin Corteel and to Tom Graves who researched the photographs for the book, to Rosie Daley, Suzanne King and Gay Notkin, who did the typing, and to yet another old-Etonian, David Roberts, who conceived and produced this book. My thanks above all to Major and Mrs Ronald Ferguson.

Gordon Honeycombe, July 1986

Text © 1986 Honeycombe House

Design, photograph selection and captions © 1986 Weidenfeld and Nicolson, TV-am and Honeycombe House
Published in Great Britain by
George Weidenfeld & Nicolson Limited
91 Clapham High Street
London SW4 7TA

All rights reserved. No part of this publication may be reproduced, stored in a retrieval system, or transmitted, in any form or by any means, electronic, mechanical, photocopying, recording or otherwise, without the prior permission of the copyright owner.

ISBN 0 297 79027 7

Printed in Great Britain by
Redwood Burn Limited, Trowbridge, Wiltshire

Prince Andrew's full coat-of-arms.

Sarah Ferguson's coat-of-arms. Both the bumble-bee, which signifies hard work, and the thistle are emblems of the Ferguson clan. The motto means: *Out of Adversity Happiness Grows*.

The engagement ring, (*title page*) partly designed by Prince Andrew and valued at about £25,000, was made by the Crown jewellers, Garrard. An oval ruby, set in a cluster of ten drop-diamonds, is mounted on an 18-carat yellow and white gold ring. Sarah wore the ring on a chain around her neck for a week before the engagement was announced.

Terence Donovan's official photograph of Prince Andrew and Sarah Ferguson before their wedding on 23 July 1986 (*frontispiece*).

CONTENTS

ACKNOWLEDGEMENTS

The Engagement 4

The Bridegroom 20

The Bride 42

The Weeks before the Wedding 62

The Wedding 70

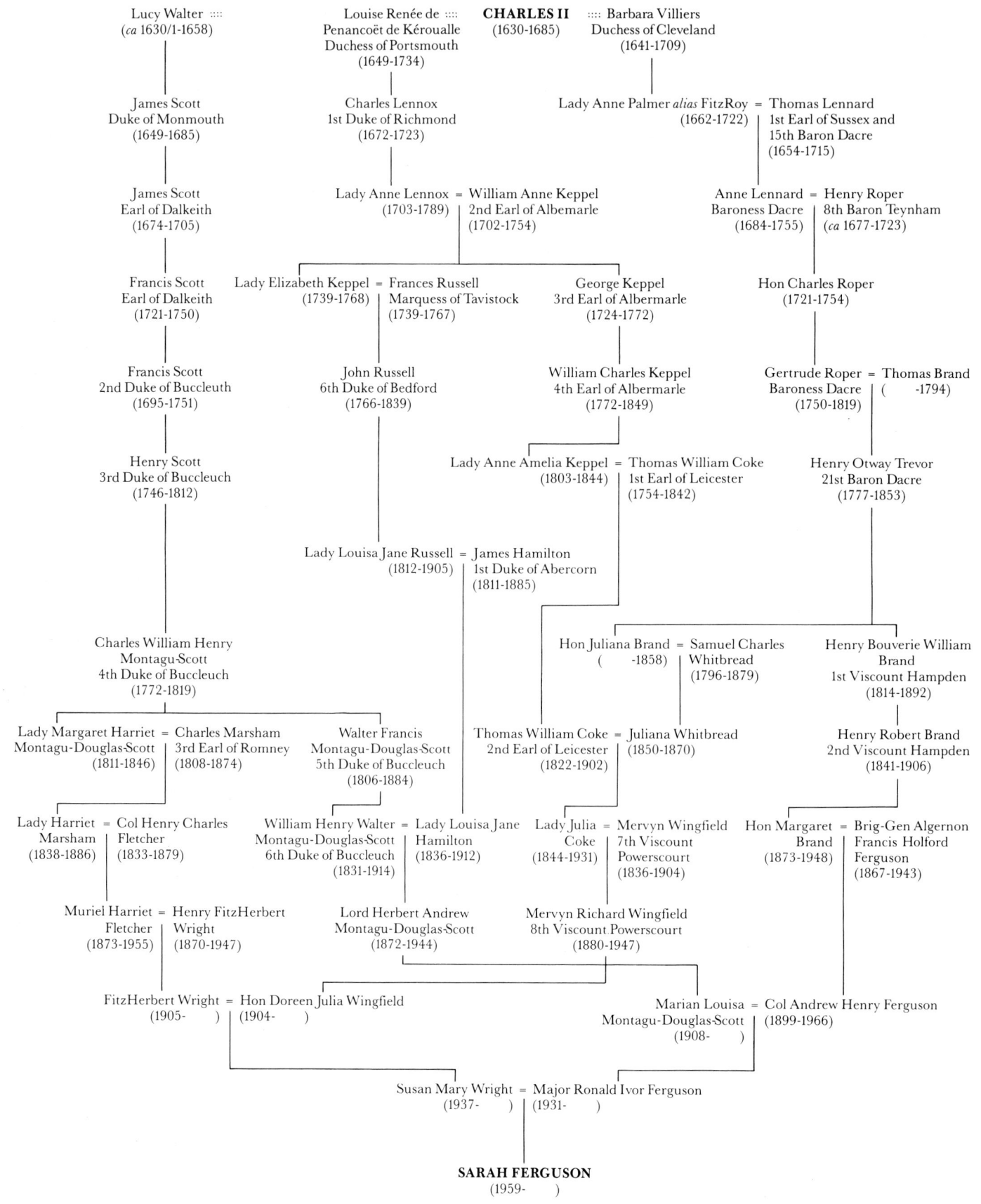

SARAH FERGUSON'S ROYAL ROOTS

PRINCE ANDREW AND SARAH FERGUSON, as with all members of the Royal Family and their courtiers of noble descent, are connected by blood. They are sixth cousins, once removed. Both have a common ancestor in William Cavendish, the 4th Duke of Devonshire (Motto: Secure by Caution). They are also related through the 1st Earl of Portland (1649–1709) and the 6th Duke of Buccleuch (Motto: I love). One of the 6th Duke's grand-daughters is Sarah's father's mother, Marian Louisa Montagu Douglas Scott, born in June 1908 and now Lady Elmhirst. She married Col. Andrew Henry Ferguson in November 1927, and when he died in August 1966, she remarried Air Marshall Sir Thomas Walker Elmhirst, in October 1968. He died in 1982.

The 1st Duke of Buccleuch was also the Duke of Monmouth, the eldest son of Charles II and a young Welsh girl, Lucy Walter, whom he met, bedded and allegedly wedded, before his 20th birthday and while both were in exile in Holland. Their first child (there was a daughter, Mary) was the first of Charles II's 13 known illegitimate children. The second, Mary, is an ancestress, via the 2nd Earl Spencer, of the present Princess of Wales. So both Diana and Sarah share an ancestor, Charles II. The 1st Earl of Harewood (1740–1820) is another common ancestor. Sarah is also a 4th cousin to the Princess of Wales via the 1st Duke of Abercorn (1811–1885), another descendant of Charles II. His seven daughters married peers. One, Lady Louisa Jane Hamilton, married the 6th Duke of Buccleuch.

Another of the 6th Duke's grand-daughters is Princess Alice, Duchess of Gloucester, born in 1901 and the widow of the Queen's uncle Prince Henry, Duke of Gloucester (younger brother of King George VI). This makes Sarah a 2nd cousin, twice removed, to Princess Alice. On her mother's side, Sarah is a seventh cousin, seven times removed, to Mrs Maria Fitzherbert, a Roman Catholic lady, twice widowed before she was 24, who secretly married Prince George, the grossly self-indulgent Prince of Wales, in 1785. The marriage was later disavowed, so that his debts of over half a million pounds could be discharged and he be able to marry a blowsy cousin, Princess Caroline of Brunswick, in 1795. He was 32, weighed 16 stone and was drunk on his wedding day. In 1820 he became King George IV. Sarah's other ancestors include the 1st Duke of Marlborough, Sir Cloudesley Shovell and Samuel Whitbread, the brewer.

Sarah is also related by marriage to the Princess of Wales. The latter's older sister, Lady Jane Spencer, married Robert Fellowes, the Queen's deputy private secretary, in 1978; his father had married a daughter of Brigadier General A. F. H. Ferguson, Sarah's great-grandfather. Both Sarah and Diana have stronger connections with the Stuart kings than Prince Charles or Prince Andrew. Sarah can trace six descents from Charles II and Diana five. Their children are and will be the most truly and royally British for over 300 years.

King Charles II.

Miss Sarah Ferguson.

THE ENGAGEMENT

It is with the greatest pleasure that
The Queen and The Duke of Edinburgh
announce the betrothal of their beloved son
The Prince Andrew to Miss Sarah Ferguson,
daughter of Major Ronald Ferguson and Mrs Hector Barrantes.

Two photo-copies of the announcement, carefully typed on Buckingham Palace notepaper, were handed to two television reporters among the few hundred people, mostly foreign tourists, crowding the railings and the entrance gate of Buckingham Palace. Sarah Brennan, the Palace press officer who had brought the copies across the forecourt from the Privy Purse door just after ten, was merely being helpful to the TV representatives of ITN and the BBC, as the news of the engagement was embargoed until 11.00 am, when it would become official. She was 'more than mildly surprised' when, back in her office, she learned that the BBC TV reporter had obliged the clamorous pressmen crowding around him by reading out the announcement – whereupon a small cheer was raised, and an excited Old English sheepdog jumped up and seized the paper.

Minutes later, at 10.07 am, the Press Association trumpeted the news on computers and tape around the world – *Andrew and Sarah engaged – Official*. But it wasn't, and at 10.26, the Press Association's 'Rush' reported a piqued Palace official as saying: *The engagement is not official. There is no announcement yet.* It was too late. It was also too late to correct an odd error below the original announcement. Instead of the day's date, 19 March, 19 *February* had been typed – coincidentally Prince Andrew's birthday.

He and his fiancée were in the sitting-room of his Palace suite enjoying a few jokes, a cup of coffee and a biscuit, with five journalists, the court correspondents of the Press Association, IRN, BBC Radio, BBC TV and ITN. Also in attendance were the Queen's Press Secretary, Michael Shea, and the Prince's private secretary, Wing-Commander Adam Wise. Sarah had said when the journalists arrived: 'I have asked Mr Shea to call you all together, so I can tell you this – it's all a hoax!' For a horrid moment more than one was taken in. Then all laughed – the ice was broken.

The second-floor suite of rooms had been Prince Charles' bachelor quarters for many years. It was here that he proposed to Lady Diana. When they married, in July 1981, Prince Andrew took over the suite. Its windows overlooked the forecourt and The Mall, but no one noticed the flurry caused by the premature announcement at the entrance gate.

Earlier, Prince Andrew had telephoned his old ship HMS *Brazen*, which was berthed at Devonport, so that the crew would hear the news before anyone else. He wanted the announcement to be broadcast on the ship at 10.45. It was – but by then it had been broadcast by every radio station, and celebrations were underway. A signal of best wishes was sent by *Brazen* to the couple and a crate of champagne broached. 'He hasn't settled his mess bill yet,' said a jocular sailor. 'So we can charge it all to him.'

Sarah Ferguson, wearing the severe, navy blue suit that would soon be seen on television, seemed to the reporters to be unaffected by the prospect of being interviewed at length and for the first time, and by her extraordinary surroundings and new status – she had moved into the Palace the

One of the official photographs taken in Buckingham Palace's Blue Drawing Room by Terence Donovan.

previous evening. She was brisk and business-like, very out-going, and displayed a good sense of humour.

At 10.30, Tom Corby, the Press Association man, was left alone with the couple to do his interview, noting what they had to say on a shorthand pad, while the two radio correspondents waited outside in the red-carpeted Chamber Floor corridor, lined with oil paintings, sofas and cabinets of priceless porcelain, with a view of the inner quadrangle. The TV interviewers were taken downstairs to await their turn.

After Corby, the couple were interviewed for radio by John Osman of the BBC and Dickie Arbiter of IRN, who had learned about the forthcoming engagement the previous morning when, after an Investiture held by the Queen in the State ballroom, Michael Shea had told him to return the next day at ten. As the microphones and recording equipment had already been set up on a low table during the coffee session, the joint radio interview proceeded straightaway.

The couple, sitting on high-backed chairs near the windows, thanked Arbiter and Osman for their congratulations. They were both cautious and uninhibited in their replies. Outside, the Life Guards rode by on their way to Horse Guards' Parade, their buglers sounding a salute, as the Queen was in residence that morning. Sarah's father, Major Ferguson, had served in the Life Guards, as had three generations of his family before him.

Sarah described the engagement ring, when asked, as being 'in the shape of a daisy' and said she hadn't found it difficult dealing with all the media attention, although she later admitted she had sometimes been 'bugged' by it. She had carried on smiling 'for Andrew's sake.' He said: 'My career plans have *not* changed . . . and Sarah has told me in no uncertain terms not to change my plans.' She said she would 'continue to work as long as it was practical' and carry on as normal. Said Andrew: 'I will go back to work and Sarah will go back to work.' He hoped the wedding would take place in the summer, although there were many matters to discuss affecting this. Of the honeymoon he said: 'That's the last thing in my thought at the moment – ' '*Our* thought,' interposed Sarah. 'Yes, you're quite right. I'm sorry,' he said, and they laughed. He thought that after the wedding they would probably live in the Palace.

After months of press speculation the engagement is official.

The whole interview lasted just over eight minutes. Goodbyes were exchanged, and the now officially engaged couple (it was after 11.00) went downstairs to the Regency Room at the ground-floor rear of the Palace, for the TV interview, which was conducted by Anthony Carthew of ITN, and Michael Cole for BBC TV. The room had a view of the terrace and gardens, and was next door to the Belgian Suite where Andrew was born.

About this time the Queen was receiving her Ambassador to Abu Dhabi, Prince Philip was at Trinity House, and Prince Charles, as Duke of Cornwall, was chairing a meeting of his Council in the Duchy of Cornwall offices in Buckingham Gate.

After the interview, about 11.45, the couple walked out onto the terrace for the press and television photo-call. It was a damp, chill and windy day, but they cheerfully posed for the photographers on the lawn. One of them asked the couple to give each other 'a peck on the cheek'. 'No,' said the Prince with a smile. 'Oh, why not?' said Sarah, and kissed him – too quickly for the photographer, who missed his chance. So they did it again. 'Did you get that?' Andrew inquired.

Soon it was over, in time for the couple, their families and millions of people elsewhere to catch the television pictures of the photo-call and the interview.

At Dummer Down Farm, in Hampshire, Sarah's stepmother, Susan Ferguson, sat enthralled before the TV set in the darkened sitting-room with a neighbour, Mrs Philippa Andrew. A snack of salmon sandwiches and glasses of wine were hardly touched. The curtains were drawn to exclude the prying gaze of press persons outside. But this couldn't blot out their voices and comments. Some had earlier called through the letter-box, saying that the engagement had been announced, hoping for a reaction. Beleaguered as she was in her own home, Mrs Ferguson remained unbothered, but as excited as anyone else about the engagement.

Major Ferguson had checked in at Heathrow Airport at 10 am before travelling by Air Canada at 11.10 to Singapore, and then on to Sydney, to see his elder daughter, Jane, and his first grand-daughter, Ayesha, now three months old. He would also be umpiring at the Royal Sydney Horse Show. Before he left, he was able to see the TV announcement of his daughter's engagement to Prince Andrew, as well as an interview he had given earlier, embargoed until then, in which he had said: 'I'm absolutely thrilled, and reasonably emotional.' Quite emotional now at his daughter's happiness, he sat alone, apart from her and his family, on the long flight to Singapore – to be overwhelmed by reporters when at last he arrived in Sydney, bearing a box of new polo-sticks for his Australian son-in-law.

Of his future son-in-law he had said: 'I think he's a very fine person. We all know he's a very professional helicopter pilot. I admire anybody who is professional at their job.' At Heathrow he had said: 'I'm absolutely delighted that Sarah is going to marry, in my opinion, a real man.'

On the afternoon of the engagement, punters struck lucky with two co-incidence bets. In the 2.30 at Worcester, the 9–4 favourite, 'St Andrew's Bay,' won – and in the 2.45 at Bristol, a greyhound called 'Falkland's Hero' (3–1) came in first. In the same race, ironically, 'Sarah's Progress' wasn't placed.

At the Palace, Sarah and her fiancé had lunch with the Queen and the Duke of Edinburgh, and at tea-time the Princess of Wales, after lunching with her husband and his Duchy Councillors at Kensington Palace, drove over to add her personal congratulations, while he visited an Exhibition of Watercolours. Later on, she and Prince Charles attended a dinner at the Royal Society of Arts, where he was presented with the Albert Medal for 1985 by his father.

That night, Andrew and Sarah dined alone in the Palace. There was much to remember of that day, and much to plan for the days ahead. If they looked back at all, it must have been to wonder at how their lives, and their view of each other had changed in the last nine months.

Although they had known each other since childhood, it was in June 1985, at lunch in Windsor Castle, that the former tomboy and tomfooling prince, saw and sensed something new about their erstwhile chum. Sarah had been invited to stay with the Royal Family at Windsor as a house-guest on three days of Royal Ascot, 18–20 June. One day, at lunch in the Castle before the carriage-drive to see the races, Sarah and Andrew sat beside each other. Over the dessert some banter resulted. He tricked her into eating chocolate profiteroles, although she was on a hypothetical diet, and she hit him. This high-spirited response evidently impressed not just Andrew, but also the Queen. Here at last was a girl of character, who

The kiss the world's press wanted.

would give as good as she got, like one of the boys, and put him down, but with good humour and affection. Despite his 'Randy' reputation, he had never, it seems, been entirely at ease with girls and tended to put on an act. No act was required with Sarah: he could be himself and not feel threatened. And he saw that she was attractive.

But Sarah was still seeing Paddy McNally, a widower, and at 48, old enough to be her father. She probably would have married him, as she might Kim Smith-Bingham. For, having committed herself to a relationship, she was faithful and loyal. But neither man apparently felt as strongly about her; and perhaps the imbalance, after two years, of their lack of devotion and commitment, made her realise that the perfect match she sought was somewhere else.

'She never lived with either of them,' Susan Ferguson once told a reporter. 'They both had homes in Switzerland, and she used to go for weeks without seeing them. Both relationships were always terribly tricky, full of goodbyes...'

Two were final. After a month with McNally in Switzerland, Sarah was back in September in London, unattached and adrift. The jovial helicopter pilot of HMS *Brazen* was also at sea, in more ways than one. After a riotous shore-leave in Florida in June, during which photographers were ejected from a nightclub, and which apparently provoked a paternal lecture at Balmoral, the unwary sailor prince was looking for an anchor, for a good friend as much as a good time. On leave in London, he invited his red-headed companion at Ascot out for a meal.

The Princess of Wales, although a close friend of Sarah, and an old friend of Andrew, was never the maker of this match. She and Sarah had become friends in the summer of 1982, a friendship that had strengthened over the next three years. But Diana, nearly two years younger than Sarah, but a Princess, wife and mother before she was 22, was the one who needed a supportive confidante, someone mature and forthright, yet sympathetic, and with a similar background. Naturally they discussed many things together. But if anyone guided Sarah, it was not Diana, but her father. She depended on him, as she had done most when her mother left home and remarried, and was most influenced by what *he* said. As was Andrew, by *his* father. The family match-makers, if any, were the middle-aged men who had matched polo-sticks for twenty years.

Andrew's naval duties often took him away on HMS *Brazen*. But he and Sarah kept in touch, by phone and letter, and met when he came up to London. Her car would be seen, parked in the forecourt, when they had a night out together. One weekend he took her to Sandringham on a pheasant shoot and to see more of his mother. The barriers fell, as in any caring relationship, and it was, it seems, in December, at a weekend house-party spent at the home of one of Andrew's friends from his Gordonstoun days that the royal romance really began. Susan Ferguson said of this time: 'There were weekends when even we didn't know where Sarah was staying. But by Christmas I knew she was very happy. She would come home positively glowing with happiness.'

Although Christmas Day was spent with their respective families, at Windsor and Dummer, Andrew and Sarah were in touch by telephone and met beforehand for an exchange of Christmas gifts. Then on Wednesday, 1 January 1986, Sarah joined the Royal Family on their annual New Year holiday at snow-bound Sandringham. She was seen about the estate with

Andrew, watching a pheasant shoot, or hand in hand as they wandered away. But she was not with his family at morning service at Sandringham church on Sunday, 5 January, as no girl-friend, unless engaged, might go with the family to church. Sarah was back at work in BCK Graphic Arts on Monday, the day Andrew, as Patron of the Jubilee Sailing Trust, paid an official visit to Wivenhoe in Essex. Few noticed that she was now wearing a ring on her left little finger – a triple Russian wedding ring, symbol of an aristocratic, unofficial, engagement.

They were together again at the weekend, which Sarah is believed to have spent in Buckingham Palace – Andrew was there at a Schools Explorers function on the Saturday – and such was the Queen's approval of the association that Sarah was again the guest of the Queen at Sandringham, staying there with Andrew on 18–19 January.

the following weekend they were at Highgrove in Gloucestershire, the country home of the Prince and Princess of Wales. As Charles was away, Diana was hostess to her friends, now publicly said to be in love after Sarah's mother, Mrs Hector Barrantes, had confided in an unfortunately talkative friend in Florida.

It was a flying visit for Andrew, as HMS *Brazen* had sailed from Devonport on Monday, 20 January, bound for Sweden and a visit to Gothenburg, where on the 30th the ship faced a demonstration at the docks by a small crowd of anti-nuclear protesters.

But then he was homeward bound, and on 4 February, *Brazen* sailed up the Thames at dawn, and berthed alongside HMS *Belfast* on an official visit to the Port of London.

In the meantime, on Sunday, 2 February, the christening of four-month-old Eliza Ferguson, daughter of Major and Mrs Ferguson, had been held in St Michael's Church, North Waltham, in Hampshire. The private ceremony was attended by the Prince and Princess of Wales – Prince Charles was a godfather; Sarah was also there.

On 4 February, the Queen and the Duke of Edinburgh visited their son on board HMS *Brazen*, where they also had lunch. She had come up to London from Sandringham, and he had flown in from Switzerland, where he had addressed a meeting of the World Wildlife Fund.

On Wednesday, 5 February, it was the turn of the Princess of Wales – Prince Charles was at Gateshead. She brought with her Prince William and Sarah Ferguson, who wore an outfit and earrings borrowed from Diana. For over an hour the party were shown around by the Captain, Richard Cobbold. It was the first official presentation, as it were, of Sarah with any member of the Royal Family, and with Prince Andrew. It was probably his idea. But the opportunity for Sarah to see over the ship where he had lived and worked for nearly two years was not to be missed. Now was the chance for press photographers to get pictures not only of Andrew and Sarah, but also of Diana and Prince William, now aged 4 (*see overleaf*). Lip-

Franklin's cartoon in the *Sun* which Sarah liked so much she asked to be given the original.

reading reporters believed they saw Diana say to Sarah: 'Keep smiling, for goodness' sake!'

Later that day, the Prince and Princess flew to Switzerland, for a ten-day skiing holiday at Klosters. The royal party stayed in a rented six-bedroom chalet at Wolfgang. On 6 February they were joined by the Duke and Duchess of Roxburghe and Sarah Ferguson.

At a photo-call staged for about 100 pressmen, Sarah's unexpected appearance in a ski-suit and a fur headband (*right, below*) upstaged that of the Princess of Wales. Cameras and reporters zoomed in on her. She dealt with questions about Andrew – 'I promise you he's not coming. He's on exercises with the Navy. Protecting our shores, I hope.' And when asked about an engagement, she said – 'Boring, boring. Let's talk about skiing.' An equerry, Major Lindsay, interposed with – 'I think that's enough.'

That night, in London, Andrew went to the theatre with some friends to see *42nd Street*, before celebrating his last night ashore with two of *Brazen*'s young officers at a favourite night club, Tramp, in Jermyn Street. They were back on board about 2.0 am; and at mid-day on Friday, 7 February, *Brazen* was towed stern-first through Tower Bridge, on her way to NATO exercises in the North Sea.

At Klosters, another photo-call, on the ski-slopes, had taken place that morning, organised so that the press could take pictures of the royal party in action and then leave them alone. Sarah and Diana shared a T-bar chair-lift to the top – Charles, his equerry, and two detectives followed. Sarah set off first down the ski-run. Charles paused to tell reporters: 'I wanted your editors to be told that Sarah was coming, but they advised against it' – they being the Palace press office. Diana retired early that day, feeling unwell, but Sarah stayed out on the slopes.

On Sunday, 9 February, the *News of the World* carried a story about Prince Philip ordering Andrew to postpone any engagement while public reaction to Sarah's so-called love affairs was assessed. And Diana, it was said, was 'battling to win royal approval for the love match'. The story was denied officially and met with laughter in Klosters, as was the *Sun*'s subsequent headline – *Di Fights Philip over Fergie*.

Although Andrew and Sarah were now parted for a fortnight, he was able to utilise a satellite link-up with an American submarine to telephone Sarah, care of NATO. Meanwhile, the Queen and the Duke of Edinburgh had left Britain on a three-week tour of Nepal, New Zealand, and Australia. Any announcement of an as yet hypothetical engagement would have to wait until the Queen's return.

Sarah returned to London with the Roxburghes on the evening of 14 February. They flew from Zurich. She was mobbed by photographers and pressmen at Heathrow, where she blithely ignored all questions about Valentine cards. She became slightly flustered, however, when her car refused to start, frustrating a quick, clean getaway. The battery was flat. The police drove her off in a patrol car to a safe haven, a police station, until her BMW was mobile again.

That weekend she went home to Dummer. When she and her father did some Saturday shopping in the village, the press were snapping at their heels, this time wanting to know what presents she had bought Andrew for his birthday on 19 February.

Back at work at BCK on Monday, but now with a police escort, she told reporters again: 'You know I can't say anything. You know how it is.' The

ratpack of press and TV crews, covering her every move in the street, now amounted to over a dozen. On the Wednesday, Andrew's birthday, she had lunch with BCK's boss, Richard Burton. That evening she was pursued by nine car-loads of desperate photographers, but eluded them in her BMW. She dined with friends – frugally, as for some time now she had been keeping an eye on her weight, eating more salads and cutting down on wine, apart from an occasional dry white wine and soda. She was a well-built 5' 8". When she could, she exercised at a gym in Chelsea, Bodys, with strenuous sessions of aerobics, and work-outs on weight machines. To maintain her ski-tan she spent time on a Uvasun bed.

On 19 February Andrew was ordered out of his bunk at 8.0 am – *Brazen* had berthed at Devonport the night before – and told to fly his Lynx on a practice flight over the frigate. As he did so, signal flags were run up that read *Happy Birthday HRH*. He was given a night's shore-leave, but probably stayed in Plymouth.

On the Friday, the press were instantly suspicious when Sarah took time off from work to have her hair done at Michaeljohn in Albemarle Street. It was learned she had a light cut, wash and dry, with highlights (for £23.50) and a £5.75 manicure. Where was she going? None could tell. And the next morning she was not at her Clapham (or, more correctly, Battersea) home. She was in Scotland, and Prince Andrew was about to propose.

They spent the weekend in the splendidly romantic, snow-girt setting of Floors Castle, near Kelso (*below*). Sarah flew to Newcastle-upon-Tyne's airport at Ponteland, using an alias, Miss Anwell, and was driven the 70 miles or so north, through Otterburn and over Carter Bar. Prince Andrew drove north from Sunderland, where HMS *Brazen* berthed on Saturday, 22 February, accompanied by a bodyguard, Geoff Padgham, who also joined in the weekend. Padgham, a Metropolitan Police Inspector, had been with Andrew since the young Prince's Canadian schooldays.

The Roxburghes left Sarah and Andrew to their own devices, and they were attended by the family butler – Hudson by name, but called John. They are believed to have taken the ducal dogs for a brisk walk along the banks of the icy Tweed and indulged in a snowball fight. At some point, possibly on Sunday night after dinner, Prince Andrew proposed, going

down on both knees, and was accepted – although Sarah told him that he could, if he changed his mind the following morning, tell her it was all a huge joke.

Sarah returned to London on Monday afternoon. Andrew drove her part of the way. An unmarked police car took her into the airport while Andrew drove on in his dark grey Jaguar to rejoin his ship in Sunderland. 'Miss Anwell' arrived at Gatwick, struggling to suppress her excitement and happiness, but unable to stop smiling.

HMS *Brazen* took Andrew back to Devonport, where the frigate docked on 28 February. In the meantime, Sarah had seen the Princess of Wales in Kensington Palace. There was no one better to confide in, with whom to share her delight. Perhaps Diana rehearsed for Sarah some of the more irritating aspects of press attention leading up to the announcement of her own engagement. The announcement of Sarah's would have to wait until after the Queen returned from Australia on 14 March. No one, apart from the favoured few, could be told until then.

It must have been frustrating, but even more so for the press, who now learned, too late, about the Scottish weekend excursion but not about the proposal. All week they hung about Mayfair and Clapham (and it was the coldest February in London for forty years). They caught her at Kensington Palace on 25 February, but then they lost her again.

On Friday, 28 February, at lunchtime, Sarah ate with a girl-friend in the Pizzeria Condotti in Mill Street. Some of the pressmen dogging her footsteps dutifully followed. A feature-writer for *Today*, Cathy Galvin, ventured into the restaurant out of the cold and sat at an adjacent table with a photographer. Indicating he had no camera, he asked if Sarah would like a drink. Sarah declined, politely: 'I must be getting back to work. I'm not being miserable or anything. Perhaps another time.' She inquired how long the press would be there. Later, when she left her office to post a letter, some pressmen and photographers, walking backwards, followed, suspecting she had devised a ruse to escape for the weekend. 'If I'd known you were there,' she told one of them, 'I'd have got you to post the letter.' She returned to the office and eventually left in a taxi summoned by an office colleague. Pressmen on motorcycles set off after her, but the taxi, anonymous amongst others, was lost in Berkeley Square. For the rest of the evening the ratpack of pressmen scurried hither and thither, checking her Battersea flat, peering into her car, at other cars leaving Buckingham Palace, up at Prince Andrew's unlit suite of rooms. Two-way radios crackled – Where had Sarah gone? But no one was to find that out.

Picture exclusives the following week showed Diana and Sarah together. They had been to see *Les Miserables* at the Palace Theatre on 6 March, and sat in the Dress Circle. Andrew, that night, was at a Royal Aero Club dinner in Piccadilly. The previous evening he had been at Selfridges, opening an exhibition of photographs of Israel by Lichfield, Snowdon and Shakerley.

That morning he had made his official departure from HMS *Brazen*. As he formally said goodbye to the officers on the flight deck, the door of the hangar lifted and a chorus-line of about thirty crewmen in funny flying gear and hats pranced out to music from *42nd Street*. They then, led by CPO Dinger Bell and to the tune of 'I'm the King of the Jungle' from the film *Jungle Book*, sang: 'I'm the Prince of the Hussy, an air-borne VIP – I'm over the top, I've had to stop, and that's what's bothering me – Oo-bi-doo, we want to be like you-oo-oo . . .' There was more. 'What a send-off!' said the Prince, who the night before had been summoned to carry out a mock mess inspection of ten Royal Marines in various items of lingerie. 'He took it very well,' said a marine. 'And everyone had a good laugh.'

On 11 March, Grania Forbes, in the *Daily Mail*, said that Andrew had proposed and been accepted and that the couple would marry in Westminster Abbey. That night they were photographed leaving the Royal Opera House, Covent Garden, after a performance of the ballet *Frankenstein* (during which they were observed to be holding hands), and a lady at the Crown jewellers, Garrard, was quoted the next day as having told a friend – 'We've got the ring!' To cap it all, the Italian proprietor of a snack bar opposite Sarah's place of work (called Queen's) and frequented by her, disclosed that she was 'very much in love'. 'I'm a very busy girl with lots of work to do,' was all Sarah would say.

Prince Andrew, released for royal duties – he had visited the SS *Great Britain* Project in Bristol on 10 March (Prince Edward's 22nd birthday) – toured an aircraft-simulator factory at Lancing, Sussex, on 12 March, before attending the London film première of *Young Sherlock Holmes*. On Sunday, 16 March he presented the singles trophies at the All-England Open Badminton Championships at Wembley.

Sarah, meanwhile, was at home in Dummer Down Farm, having gone there on Thursday. But with the help of her father, she eluded the press posse on Saturday and drove to Windsor Castle. The Queen and the Duke of Edinburgh had returned to England on the morning of Friday, 14 March. She was told then about the engagement by her son, and congratulated them both the next day. Both families met at the Castle that night, apart from Susan Ferguson, who remained at home with her children.

On Monday, 17 March, Sarah had lunch with her father in Claridge's. Now attended in the street by two uniformed policemen and a plain-clothes detective, as well as several dozen photographers and reporters, she took a short-cut through Sotheby's to reach the hotel. He and Sarah were in high spirits, and happily smiled for the cameras. He drove her to the Ritz, where she watched a fashion show. Later, she paid a brief visit to Buckingham Palace, before returning to her Clapham flat.

The mob of pressmen was even larger the following day. Sarah still continued to smile and say nothing, only denying that there was any significance in the sailor-style suit she wore, decked with three ornamental flags. It was Budget Day, and no day for anything other than financial announcements, including a penny off Income Tax. Sarah arrived at work at 10.30 am and two hours later left to have lunch with Susan Ferguson in the Westbury Hotel. 'This is my wicked stepmother!' she said laughing, presenting Mrs Ferguson to the press. Receiving a gift of red roses she said: 'I'm the last person in the world who needs cheering up today!'

Later that day, 18 March, she moved into Buckingham Palace.

Although her life had been in part a preparation for what was to come, no one could have foretold that little Sarah, 'Fergie', the freckled, red-haired child, teenager, girl and young woman, would one day marry a Prince. Not even she, even six months ago. Now the door of her Battersea home had shut behind her. Others would open, but nothing would ever be the same.

On Wednesday, 19 March 1986, her engagement was announced, albeit a little early, to the second eldest son of the Queen.

TELEVISION INTERVIEW

given by Prince Andrew and Sarah Ferguson on 19 March 1986

Interviewers: Michael Cole (BBC TV) and Anthony Carthew (ITN)

COLE Could you tell us please, first of all, how long ago you decided to marry?

ANDREW I asked Sarah some weeks ago, and Sarah actually said 'Yes' which – (SARAH: Surprised him) It surprised me. She did say also, which is a little anecdote for you – she said: 'If you wake up tomorrow morning, you can tell me it's all a huge joke.' I didn't.

SARAH (*laughs*) So we're sitting here.

CARTHEW You started from a meeting at Ascot and then everything developed from there in a way. When did you both know that it was the real thing?

ANDREW Again, very difficult to answer. But I think that ... probably at the end of last year, before Christmas perhaps. And then it sort of – (SARAH: Carried on from there) Carried on from there – after Christmas, at Sandringham and then beyond that.

CARTHEW What first impressions did you have of one another then?

SARAH (*looking at Andrew*) Very good friends.

ANDREW 'A' – very good friends, and 'B' – well, it was at lunch, wasn't it, that we – (SARAH: Yes). We were made to sit next door to each other at Ascot.

SARAH Yes, and he made me eat chocolate profiteroles, which I didn't want to eat at all.

ANDREW (*laughing*) I then didn't have any – so I got hit (SARAH: Very hard). And it started from there.

SARAH I was meant to be on a diet (*looks at Andrew, both laugh*).

CARTHEW And that was the basis of a romance?

SARAH (*with a laugh*) Yes.

ANDREW There are always humble beginnings. It's got to start somewhere. But, I mean, we've known each other since we were four or five ... About 1983, we were staying at various house-parties around the country during part of '83 and '84, and it was at Ascot that, as it were, the whole thing, as you say, took off. But it wasn't at Ascot week, it wasn't at *Ascot* as such, that we realised that there was anything in it. It was later on.

SARAH No. Exactly.

COLE I think you said that when you met the right girl, it would probably come like a lightning bolt?

ANDREW You're not the first person who has asked me this question today ... I'm at a loss really to say – I mean, I don't think that Sarah is a thunderbolt.

SARAH Nor am I a streak of lightning. Nor is he, I don't think. (*Both laugh*)

COLE Could you tell us what you like about each other?

ANDREW Oh! (*They look at each other and smile*)

SARAH Wit! (*She laughs*) Charm! (*Looks at Andrew*)

ANDREW Yes, probably ... (*looks at her*). And the red hair.

SARAH And the good looks. (*Nudges him*) Sorry! (*Laughs*)

CARTHEW Could we – ?

ANDREW (*interrupting; at Sarah*) I'm watching carefully.

SARAH I'm going to be hit! (*giggles*)

CARTHEW Could we have a rather more lingering look at the ring? I mean, how did you find time to go out and buy it?

ANDREW (*holding Sarah's hand; both examine the ring*) Well, very fortunately, I didn't actually have to go *out* and buy it! Somebody very kindly came in with some suggestions, and it was made, very kindly, by some very nice engineers, I think. (SARAH: *Engineers!*) I don't think they'd like to be called engineers. (SARAH: Definitely!) But I'm not quite sure what you call jewellery engineers.

SARAH (*laughs*) Jewellers!

ANDREW Jewellers.

COLE Miss Ferguson, how would you describe that lovely ring?

SARAH Stunning. Red. I wanted a ruby. I didn't *want* it – I'm very lucky to have it. But certainly it's a lovely stone, and I've got red hair too.

ANDREW It was, er, again it's something that we discussed in the last few weeks. And we came to the mutual conclusion that red was probably the best colour for Sarah, and, er, that's how we came to the choice of the ruby. And then the extra bits around the outside – we wanted something that was slightly unconventional, and I think we've got something there.

SARAH Very original. (*Looking at Andrew, helpfully*) I think, Andrew, you actually designed it, didn't you?

ANDREW I helped in its design.

CARTHEW What – you mean with sketches and things?

ANDREW Er, well, we did sketch *some* of it. And I found a suggestion in another selection of rings that I was given, and I then asked them to change – I'm not quite sure what the shape was of the original that I drew, but they looked like rugby balls, little tiny ones. And these are drops rather than rugby balls (*holding Sarah's hand and displaying the ring*).

SARAH Thank goodness for that. (*Laughs*) I'd hate to wear a rugby ball around my hand. (*Both laugh*)

COLE Can you tell us about the proposal – where and when it took place?

SARAH (*looking at Andrew*) Scotland.

ANDREW It was some weeks ago, staying privately in Scotland. Er, and I'll go no further than saying that.

COLE Could I ask you then, Miss Ferguson – do you remember what he said?

SARAH Absolutely! (*Laughs*) But I'm not telling *you*! (*All laugh*)

COLE Did he go down on one knee, in the approved fashion?

ANDREW (*They look at each other*) No. Both. That I will tell you – both.

SARAH Yes, both. Both knees.

COLE And you, of course, very formally asked your prospective father-in-law for Miss Ferguson's hand in marriage?

ANDREW Yes. That was also fairly nerve-wracking, knowing Major Ronald from a very long time ago and at the polo. And I asked him this weekend, as well as Her Majesty.

COLE What *was* the Queen's reaction?

ANDREW (*with his arms folded*) Overjoyed. Very happy. Very pleased, and beyond that – what else? I mean, just as a delighted parent, I think.

SARAH As, indeed, was my father.

CARTHEW There was no phrase using the words 'settling down' when she said 'Congratulations'?

ANDREW (*with mock mystification*) How do you mean – 'settling down'? (*Sarah laughs*)

CARTHEW Well, becoming a married man and –

ANDREW Oh, gosh! You mean *that* way. No, no. I mean, I don't see that there's anything settling in it. It's a mighty upheaval for most people, and I think it will be an upheaval for both of us, in that we've got to come to terms with life as it will continue.

SARAH But we're a good team anyway. (*Looking at him*) I think – aren't we?

ANDREW Yes, I think that's the saving grace – the fact that in the last nine months we've discovered that we work very well together.

SARAH We're good friends – good team. Quite happy – very happy. (*Looking at him but he adds nothing*).

COLE Miss Ferguson, could I ask you how you're going to cope with this new role and at the same time be a Navy wife?

SARAH I'm going to enjoy it immensely. I think I'm going to cope, with the help of Andrew here.

ANDREW I think it's worth saying that I have no plans to change my Naval career, on the advice of Sarah.

SARAH Very strong advice (*glancing at him. He smiles slightly*).

ANDREW We discussed it at some length, and for the foreseeable future I will be maintaining my Naval career as it is at the moment. And Sarah is quite prepared to put up with that ... I know how difficult it is, talking to other Naval colleagues of mine – what it's like to be married to a Naval officer – because we do spend such a long time away.

SARAH And also – I've got a job to do too, and I'm going to keep on working. And so I think it's going to be very good.

CARTHEW You think it will be possible to keep on working?

SARAH Absolutely....

CARTHEW Have you, in the course of this last rather difficult month or so, had advice from the Princess of Wales, who went through much the same thing?

SARAH Mmn – the Princess of Wales and I are extremely good friends, and we naturally talk about a lot of different subjects.

CARTHEW Like dealing with the media?

SARAH (*shrugs*) Lots of different subjects. (*Smiles*)

ANDREW Yes, I think that's probably the best way of answering that. (SARAH: We are very very good friends.) I mean, there are so many different, differing ideas about how to handle yourself, that you can't take one person's advice all the time.

SARAH (*quietly*) Although there is no one better than the Princess of Wales.

COLE What sort of wedding would you like to have?

ANDREW Er ... As in 'red, white or blue'? (*All laugh*) I hope a London wedding, and I hope a white wedding. Sarah is already charging around looking for a dress, or looking for ideas. Beyond that...

SARAH Have you got your dress?

ANDREW Yes, I've got my dress, thank you. (SARAH: Oh, good!) Yes, yes. I'm not so sure that it will fit. (*They laugh*) But anyway – No, the plans are still up in the air because now, of course, we go on into the planning stage, and the summer schedule is a very tight one, and I would very much like it to be in the summer. So would Sarah. Sarah more so, because I think that we –

SARAH (*agreeing*) Mmn – get on with it.

ANDREW And get it out of the way. But of course the summer schedule is very tight and I would hope – sometime perhaps in July or August. If it's not possible to do it in July and August, then I think I would –

SARAH (*breaking in*) We would.

ANDREW We would. Sorry. I've got to get used to this 'We' business.

SARAH (*looking at him with a smile*) I know. It's difficult, isn't it? 'We' – Okay?

ANDREW We. Yes – right. Otherwise the fall-back is some time in the autumn.

COLE Because it *has* been a bit of a whirlwind, hasn't it?

SARAH (*interrupting*) Definitely not!

ANDREW I certainly wouldn't consider it a whirlwind at all. It may be a whirlwind to *some* people – because of course, I suppose the media only discovered about it in –

SARAH In January.

ANDREW In January, and December – just after Christmas. There's quite a lot that went on before. In fact, more than what went on afterwards.

COLE What are you plans between now and the wedding?

SARAH Hard work.

ANDREW Hard work. I've got a course to do.

SARAH And I've got a job to do.

ANDREW So, we shall be getting on with it. The course that I'm going to do finishes at the beginning of June, so I will have time to sit down and plan the wedding and the arrangements afterwards.

CARTHEW Looking to the future a little. You come, both of you, from fairly large families. Would you like to repeat that pattern? Would you like to have quite a lot of children?

SARAH Mmn. (*They look at each other and smile*)

ANDREW I don't know really. I mean – what do you say? (*Looking at her*)

SARAH I don't know. What do *you* say? (*Smiling*) Shall we have a vote?

ANDREW I think we haven't actually – I mean, that's something until we get married, that we haven't even sort of thought about. There's an awful lot to think about in the next, whatever it is until we get married.

SARAH It would be fun to have quite a few, wouldn't it?

ANDREW I agree. I think it would be quite fun. But again – numbers, size and all the rest of it, is still way way in the future.

SARAH It has yet to be decided.

CARTHEW Notionally, it's a good idea then?

ANDREW Yes.

COLE Could I put a final question to you, Miss Ferguson? How do you feel about your new title – because after your marriage you'll be known as 'Princess Andrew'? (*They laugh*)

ANDREW (*to her*) You can answer that one.

SARAH I'm going to. How do I feel about my new title? (ANDREW: Change of name) Change of name. A great honour. Much looking forward to carrying it out – whatever I'm supposed to do. That's it, I think...

CARTHEW Well, may I, on behalf of ITN and the BBC, offer you our best wishes and every happiness for the future.

ANDREW Thank you very much indeed.

SARAH Thank you very much indeed.

THE BRIDEGROOM

The Queen's third child and second son was born at 3.30 pm on Friday, 19 February 1960; she was nearly 34. The birth took place in the gilt splendour of the Belgian Suite, overlooking the wintry rear terrace, the Palace gardens and lake. The baby weighted 7lb 3oz and was the first child since 1857 to be born to a reigning monarch. Wearing a robe of Honiton lace, first worn by Queen Victoria's first son, he was christened in the Palace's Music Room by the Archbishop of Canterbury, Dr Fisher, and given the names Andrew Albert Christian Edward.

Andrew's nanny (*right*) was Mabel Anderson: later, he called her 'Mamba'. Daughter of a Liverpool policeman, and a Scot, she had first been employed (through an ad in a nursing magazine) to take care of the infant Princess Anne. Firmness and fresh air were her watchwords. But when it was Mabel's night out, the Queen bathed Andrew herself and put him to bed. Prince Charles, aged 11, was away at Cheam when his brother was born; Anne, aged 9, still lived in the Palace.

Although Andrew's father and mother had determined that their third child (and their fourth, Prince Edward) should be brought up as far as possible away from press and public, he made an appearance before the cameras on the Queen Mother's 60th Birthday, and on the Buckingham Palace balcony after the Trooping the Colour ceremony in June 1961 (*below left and far right*) marking the Queen's official birthday. He was a jolly baby, full of smiles, and rarely cried.

As a child (*right*), Andrew was noisy and rumbustious; but although he was naughty, he was never nasty. He was known by the staff as 'Andy Pandy' and 'the young imp'. His father, whom he called 'Papa', taught him to swim in the Palace indoor swimming-pool, and both enjoyed various knockabout games of football and cricket in the Palace gardens and sometimes, when Andrew was on his own, in Palace corridors.

After Prince Charles went to Gordonstoun in 1962, and Princess Anne to Benenden in 1963, Andrew saw much less of his older brother and sister. But he acquired a younger brother and companion when Prince Edward was born in March 1964 (*above*).

When Andrew was 5, Catherine Peebles, who had been the older children's governess, was given the task of continuing his basic education begun by the Queen, who taught him the alphabet, numbers and how to tell the time. Miss Peebles was known as 'Mispy'. Andrew had four companions, two boys and two girls, and they met in the old nursery above the Palace balcony – furnished now with desks, a blackboard, world map and a globe. Viscount Linley joined the class later on. The rudiments of dancing, the piano, skating and sailing, were taught elsewhere – dancing by Madame Vacani, who had taught the Queen as a child. There was also gym in Chelsea Barracks, and games at the Brigade of Guards' cricket ground outside the Chelsea Pensioners' Hospital.

In 1968, Andrew was for several months a rather boisterous wolf cub with the 1st Marylebone Cub Scout pack, who met weekly in the Palace grounds. For the first time he mixed with commoners, including the sons of a policeman, a Pakistani shopkeeper, and an upholsterer. His exuberance found a useful outlet. At other times it led to practical jokes, like tying together the bootlaces of immobile sentries, tobogganing down Palace staircases on a silver tray, ringing bells for maid-service when none was required, and emptying a bubble-bath bottle into the inlet of the Windsor Castle swimming-pool. Remarked the Queen: 'He isn't always a little ray of sunshine about the home.'

(*Below*) Andrew and Sarah both aged 10, and Jane Ferguson (with a pony-tail). Their families often met at polo weekends.

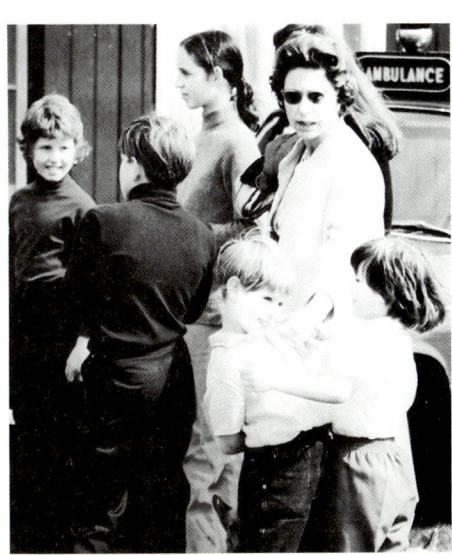

At weekends, Andrew was often a spectator at polo matches in Windsor Great Park (*right*). Major Ferguson, his future father-in-law, receives a trophy from Lord Mountbatten in 1967.

In September 1968, Andrew went as a boarder to a preparatory school, Heatherdown, near Ascot. Unlike his elder brother, Charles, the rough and tumble, the afternoon emphasis on sporting activities, suited Andrew's competitive, extrovert character. He shared a dormitory with six boys, and was treated, apart from an attendant detective, as one of them, with the bonus of pocket money and occasional weekends at home. He was joined at Heatherdown at the end of 1970 by his cousin, the Earl of St Andrews, the eldest son of the Duke and Duchess of Kent, and later by his younger brother, Edward. Andrew was at Heatherdown for five years. He passed his Common Entrance and played in the First XI and the First XV. He had received private coaching in cricket at Lords, and tennis lessons from Dan Maskell. His father taught him to shoot.

It was announced on 29 May 1973 – on the same day as the engagement of Princess Anne and Captain Mark Phillips – that Prince Andrew would go to Gordonstoun School (*right*) in September. He was accompanied by a second cousin, Amanda Knatchbull. Girls had been admitted to the school the previous year – now 30 had joined the boys. Gordonstoun's motto is *Plus est en vous* (More is in you). For a time Andrew wanted everyone to know, now he was no longer boss of Heatherdown, that he was more special than the others – no less than a son of the Queen. He swaggered (and sniggered) a lot. A contemporary said: 'It was soon knocked out of him. The ribbings he got were unmerciful and he caught on fast.' A teacher commented: 'He's a very tough and independent fellow. If anyone tries to take the mickey out of him, he fights back. He's just as good with the verbalistics as with his fists.' But he was frequently penalised for larking about and ragging. But he was also a quick and eager student, avid to know. In the summer of 1976 he not only got into the First XI but took six 'O' levels with comparative ease. Discos, a regular occurrence at Gordonstoun, made Andrew happily aware of an unsuspected asset, his maturing good looks, and the effect he had on girls. One, aged 14, said: 'He's a great dancer. I've danced with him many times. But he dances with a lot of girls. Just when you think you are getting somewhere with him, he goes off with somebody else.' That wasn't the only drawback. Another girl found his detective's presence 'a real passion-killer.' The detective's surname was Topless.

The 21st Olympic Games, held in Montreal in July 1976, were opened by the Queen and Prince Philip, three months after her 50th birthday. Princess Anne and her husband were in the British Equestrian team. Andrew flew out to join them. His official companion at the various events, visits and receptions was Sandi Jones, aged 16, daughter of a retired Canadian colonel. The ten-day visit was a personal success for the tall young Prince. His natural vitality, handsome figure, and easy confidence won him admirers, and he thrived on their esteem.

Andrew spent the first five months of 1977 in Canada, going to an exclusive, long-established school, Lakefield College, some 70 miles north of Toronto. The College, which had an exchange scheme with Gordonstoun, had been visited by Prince Philip in 1969. Lakefield and Canada would do as much for Andrew as Geelong and Australia had done for Charles. He said soon after his arrival: 'The school is quite excellent, and so are all the facilities . . . The boys here are terrific, really great. They are different from the chaps in England, because they have a different outlook from a different country. On top of that, everyone in Canada is incredibly friendly. You can say that life out here is very good indeed.' At Lakefield, Andrew learned to play ice-hockey – 'He was pretty good. He quite surprised me,' said the head-boy. 'He was quite vicious too, and you need to be a bit vicious to be good at the game.' He also ski-ed and in the summer term played rugby (as full-back), hockey and cricket. Girls gathered to watch him play, some wearing T-shirts saying *Andy for King*. The boys had begun by calling him 'Andy'. When he left Wakefield, it was 'Randy Andy'. In the Easter holiday, Andrew went ski-ing with the Canadian Prime Minister, Pierre Trudeau, his wife and children. He also saw some more of Sandi Jones. He had invited her to a school dance in January. Now she spent a few days with him in Toronto although, as she admitted later, there wasn't much romancing under the eye of his bodyguards. 'We managed to give them the slip on occasions,' she said. 'Andrew can be extremely resourceful.' She saw him again when he returned to Canada for a summer holiday.

Prince Andrew took part in a Lakefield school production of *Oliver* playing Mr Brownlow (*kneeling*).

Andrew was in England for the major celebrations marking the Queen's Silver Jubilee. He attended the Thanksgiving Service in St Paul's Cathedral on 2 June 1977. On his return to Canada, Andrew paid official visits to Alberta and British Columbia, touring several National Parks; he joined the World Wildlife Fund. Algonquin Indians dubbed him 'Heir of the Earth'; star-struck girls thought him 'cute'. Prince Charles, who met up with him at the Calgary Stampede, described him as 'the one with the Robert Redford looks'.

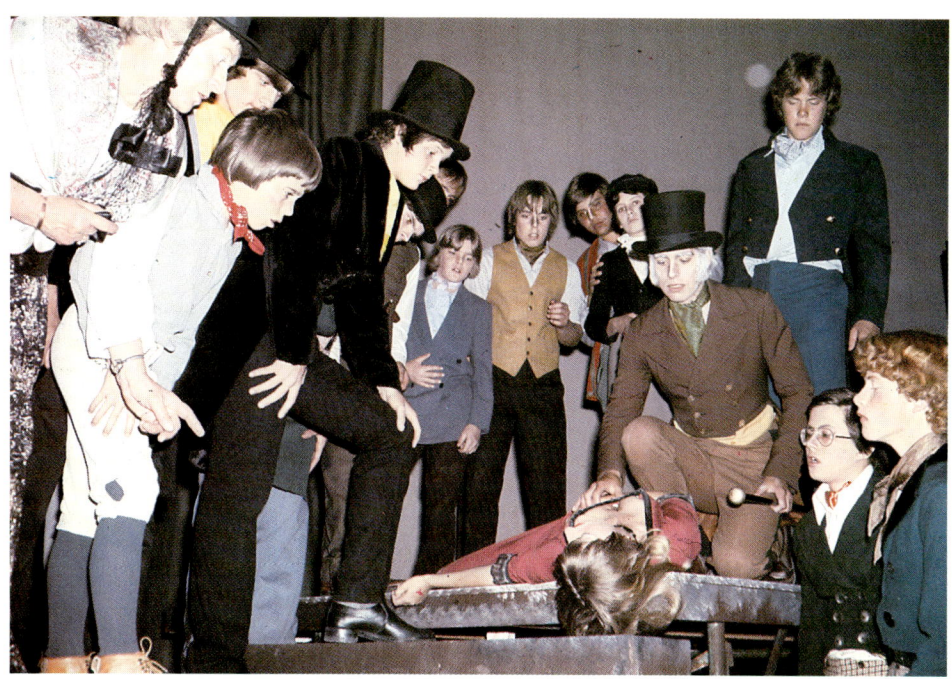

In July 1977, Andrew flew north to Yellowknife, on the Great Slave Lake, and then on to Point Lake and the Coppermine River, joining a small canoeing expedition from Lakefield College down 300 miles of river to the sea. He shared a two-man canoe with his former headmaster, Terry Guest. For two weeks they journeyed through rough country, through rapids and swamps, crossing the Arctic Circle. The expedition ended at Coppermine on the Coronation Gulf, within sight of the Duke of York archipelago (*above*).

In August, Andrew once again went sailing at Cowes (*left*). Then he travelled in the Royal Yacht *Britannia* on a family visit to Northern Ireland, his first, where he attended the opening of a new university at Coleraine in North Antrim. After that, he relaxed at Balmoral, taking part in the family's annual outing to the Braemar Highland Games. Then it was back to Gordonstoun, where Edward was starting his first term.

There were now 120 girls among the 450 pupils. Some became known as 'Andrew's Harem'. A few were invited to stay at Windsor, Balmoral and Sandringham as guests of the Queen.

On 19 February 1978, Andrew was 18. His parents' birthday present was a blue Triumph Dolomite Sprint. Within the Household and among the staff, he would from now on be officially addressed as 'Prince Andrew.' He was also now on the Civil List, and would receive a £20,000-a-year grant from Parliament. But the Queen had decided that he would receive no more than £600 a year, the rest being invested until he became a full-time Royal, or married. All the Queen's children were brought up not to be wasteful or extravagant. Andrew is said to be her most favoured son, as he resembles his father in many ways. On his 18th birthday the press praised his self-confidence, dynamism and evident charisma (*right*).

That Easter, both Charles and Andrew won their parachute wings. They trained at No. 1 Parachute Training School, at Brize Norton in Oxfordshire, then jumped from a balloon 1,000 feet above the ground. Andrew's jump from a Hercules Transport plane, at the same height, took place above South Cerney airfield in Gloucestershire on 19 April. The lines became twisted, but he was able to disentangle them, landing safely in the dropping-zone after a 49-second fall. He said: 'Of course I was nervous. If you're not nervous, you'll do something stupid ... I'm dead keen to get up again. Parachuting is a feeling I would never have wanted to miss.' The next day he did another jump, carrying a 55-pound army pack. Andrew was awarded his RAF parachute insignia and certificate on 21 April 1978.

In August 1978, when the Queen and Prince Philip opened the Commonwealth Games in Edmonton, Alberta, Andrew and Edward joined them. Andrew also visited Ottowa and British Colombia. Back in Britain, at Balmoral, the decision was probably made that Andrew would not, as some had thought, go to university (to Clare College, Cambridge), when he left Gordonstoun but enter the Royal Navy. He applied for a 12-year commission as a helicopter pilot. In December, he went to the RAF Officers' Selection Centre at Biggin Hill for three days of tests, obtaining 'a glowing report'. Then he went to Lee-on-Solent, to HMS Daedalus, the Fleet Air Arm establishment opposite Portsmouth, for further tests and interviews. In due course he learned that he had been accepted as a trainee helicopter pilot, and would begin as such in Dartmouth in September 1979. Five years later he told David Frost : 'I've always wanted to fly and I've always wanted to go to sea. I've always had an affinity with water – it's part of everyone – we *are* an island nation. I live to fly and I live to fly from the sea.' He learned to fly at RAF Benson, south of Oxford, his first solo flight, in an RN Chipmunk, being on 13 April 1979.

In his last year at Gordonstoun, Andrew was head of his house. He played First XI hockey, captained the cricket XI and gained 'A' levels in History, English, Economics and Political Sciences. He left Gordonstoun on 17 July 1979; he was 19½.

Two days after he left Gordonstoun, Andrew went with his parents on their 2½-week tour of African Commonwealth countries, flying out in an RAF VC10, specially converted, to Tanzania. The tour nearly never took place. A new state had just been created, Zimbabwe-Rhodesia, theoretically ruled by the black majority now in power. But guerrilla warfare was being waged across the border with Zambia, and the new Conservative leader, Margaret Thatcher, who became Prime Minister in May 1979, affected to advise the Queen about whether the tour should go ahead. The Queen was not amused, as head of the Commonwealth, by any such advice. The tour was a personal diplomatic triumph for her, and concluded with a Commonwealth Heads of Government Conference in Lusaka (*right*).

Andrew, Edward, and their mother, at lunch in Balmoral on Bank Holiday Monday, 27 August, were shattered by the news of the death of Earl Mountbatten. He and his family, on holiday in Ireland, were out sailing in Donegal Bay when an IRA remote-controlled bomb blew up the boat. Two of the family, and a local boy, were also killed, and three others badly injured. Lord Mountbatten's funeral service, pre-planned by himself, took place (*above*) in Westminster Abbey on 5 September 1979. It was Andrew's first experience of such a solemn state occasion, and for the first time in public he was seen in naval uniform, as a midshipman. His father, Mountbatten's nephew, and Prince Charles, also wore naval uniforms – as Admiral of the Fleet and Commander RN respectively. Mountbatten himself, and his father, Prince Louis of Battenberg, had both been First Sea Lords.

A week after Mountbatten's funeral, on 12 September 1979, Andrew arrived at the Royal Naval College at Dartmouth to begin his basic naval training. The royal tradition of service and interest in the Navy goes back to Henry VIII, who created the Navy Board, the post of Lord High Admiral, and the largest and most efficient fleet since the days of King Alfred. The Stuart kings took a personal interest in the development of the Navy and ship-building – Charles II and his brother, James II, were the first royal yachtsmen who went sailing for pleasure. The Hanoverian kings were not too keen on the sea, but the last of them, William IV (1765–1837), known as the Sailor King, went to sea when he was 13, fought in several naval battles, and rose to become a boisterous Admiral of the Fleet and the last Lord High Admiral. Queen Victoria's second son, Prince Alfred, Duke of Edinburgh (1844–1900) spent 35 years in the Navy, also becoming Admiral of the Fleet. George V, a naval cadet before he was 13, was in the Navy for 15 years; and three of *his* sons, who became Edward VIII, George VI, and the Duke of Kent, all went to the College at Dartmouth. George VI, as a 20-year-old gunnery officer, served in 1916 on a battleship during the Battle of Jutland, the most destructive naval engagement of the First World War. Prince Charles passed through Dartmouth in 1971, already a Flight Lieutenant in the RAF.

During his training, he was posted to the aircraft carrier HMS *Hermes* with 19 other midshipmen on 22 February 1980, just after his 20th birthday. It was his first sea tour, and was enlivened by shore parties and visits in Florida and Bermuda. At the end of it, in March, he went through a tough Royal Marine commando course at Lympstone in Devon, obtaining the coveted green beret. At the passing-out parade at Dartmouth, on 2 April 1980, the Queen took the salute. Between April and October 1980, Andrew went on several courses. On his time off, he was to be seen in London with various friends, some from school, others from aristocratic and courtiers' families, having fun at Tramps in Jermyn Street and at Wedgies in King's Road. He became friendly with a Miss United Kingdom, Carolyn Seaward. She was later replaced by two models, Gemma Curry (whom he took to the 50th birthday party in the Ritz of his aunt, Princess Margaret), and Miss Curry's cousin, Kim Deas. On *Britannia* during Cowes Week in August 1980 his companion (no more) was Lady Diana Spencer.

On 9 November 1980, Andrew arrived at the Royal Naval Air Station at Culdrose in Cornwall, for further training on fixed-wing aircraft and on Gazelle helicopters. His 21st birthday was celebrated in Windsor Castle with a family dinner-party on Thursday, 19 February 1981. The engagement between his older brother and Lady Diana was about to be announced. Andrew obtained a brief extension of his leave to be with them on the day of the official engagement, Tuesday 24 February. After lunching with them and his mother that day at Buckingham Palace, he watched from a window as Charles and Diana appeared together in the gardens and posed for the world's press.

On 2 April 1981, Midshipman The Prince Andrew won not just his wings as a helicopter pilot, but a silver salver, the Louis Newark Trophy, for coming top of his course. They were presented at Culdrose by his proud father, Prince Philip, another royal helicopter pilot (*below*). The salver, won on merit, was gained by his 'genuine aptitude for helicopter flying and a determination to succeed.' Andrew then began the long months of operational and advanced training on Sea King helicopters, during which, in the Firth of Clyde, in September, he piloted the helicopter that rescued a seaman who had been swept off a surfaced submarine by rough seas.

On Saturday, 13 June 1981, Andrew accompanied Lady Diana to Trooping the Colour on Horse Guards Parade (*above left*); and on 19 June, over 600 guests attended a ball at Windsor Castle, given in belated celebration of Andrew's 21st birthday, and of his father's 60th birthday (on 10 June). In the days before the wedding of Prince Charles and Lady Diana, (*below left and above*) who was 20 on 1 July, Andrew went to his brother's stag-night dinner-party at White's Club in St James's on 22 July; watched him play polo for England II against Spain at Smith's Lawn, Windsor (and win) on Sunday, 26 July; attended a dinner-dance on the Monday night given by the Queen at Buckingham Palace for the family's closest friends and wedding guests, most of whom, on the eve of the wedding, watched a spectacular firework display in Hyde Park backed by music, choirs and guns – the biggest display of its kind in Britain for over 200 years.

Prince Andrew, and his brother Edward, were Prince Charles's 'supporters' at the royal wedding on Wednesday, 29 July, Andrew carrying the wedding ring. Dressed in his midshipman's uniform, and wearing his 1977 Jubilee Medal, he accompanied his older brother to St Paul's Cathedral in the 1902 State Postillion Landau. After the marriage service, which began at 11 am, Andrew returned to Buckingham Palace with his grandmother, the Queen Mother. On the last of the four appearances that the whole family made on the balcony before the wedding breakfast, it was he who urged Prince Charles to kiss the bride. Before the bridal couple left the Palace, at 4.20 pm, Andrew tied bunches of blue and silver balloons to the back of the Landau, as well as a placard – on it, using lipstick, he and Edward drew a heart and an arrow, and the words *Just Married*.

Commissioned as a Sub-Lieutenant on 1 September 1981, Andrew (*left*) was posted on 27 October to 820 Squadron on one of the Royal Navy's largest and newest ships, the 19,500 ton aircraft-carrier HMS *Invincible*, based at Portsmouth. He flew there from Culdrose on 21 January 1982. The previous month, on 8 December, he made his first public speech, a jokey one, delivered with great aplomb, at a dinner in the Hilton Hotel celebrating the 100th rugby match between Oxford and Cambridge (*below left*).

On 5 April 1982, Andrew went to war. *Invincible* was one of 40 ships sent as a Task Force to the Falkland Islands to oust the Argentinian forces that had occupied the islands. As a co-pilot of the 10 Sea Kings on board, he was just one of 1,200 men, 'one of the crowd', although he had a cabin of his own. He was known as 'H' and kept fit by pounding around the flight deck, four times round being about a mile. He said later: 'You tend to become a sort of zombie. All you do is eat, sleep and fly. I had an awful lot of time to myself' His CO, the commander of 820 Squadron, said: 'I will order Prince Andrew into battle, as I would any of my other pilots. He gets the same work to do, and he gets no quarter . . .'

The Sea Kings were used to search for enemy submarines, to ferry supplies from ship to ship, and to carry troops ashore. They were also used as decoys for Exocet missiles – confusing the missiles by hovering near the carrier and presenting themselves as radar targets enlarged by the scattering of 'chaff' (bomb-bursts of silver paper). Two Exocets aimed at the *Invincible* on 25 May were diverted onto and struck a large supply ship, *Atlantic Conveyor*. 'It was something I will never forget,' said Andrew later. 'It was quite horrific.' His helicopter then took part in the rescue of 25 survivors of the doomed ship from a life-raft in heavy seas. When HMS *Sheffield* was hit, he confessed: 'One really did not know which way to turn and what to do... I was fairly frightened then.' But the worst moments for him were when the carrier itself was under attack – 'You are in your anti-flash protective head and arm clothing and someone has told you to hit the deck. You have to wait and lie there and only wait and hope' – and when British Sea Wolf missiles mistakenly zoned in on him – 'Sea Wolfs locked onto our helicopter three times while we were hovering. It really makes the hair stand up on the back on your neck.' Later he said: 'I think being shot at is the most character-forming thing of one's life.'

HMS *Invincible* returned to Portsmouth on 17 September 1982, after the longest time at sea, 166 days, ever spent by an aircraft-carrier. It was a triumphant, emotional occasion. A red rose was given to every man on board as he stepped ashore. Tried and tested by battle, he had achieved more than his elder brother, and had even been freed from the apprehension that, should Charles have a fatal accident, he would become heir to the throne. For in June a son had been born to Charles and Diana. Andrew was his own man at last. The Sailor Prince was welcomed back to Balmoral by being hauled in a rowing-boat through the gates of the Castle, in the rain.

At the Remembrance Day ceremony at the Cenotaph on 14 November 1982, Andrew laid a wreath, a personal tribute, in memory of all those who had died during the Falklands Campaign. He was now back with 820 Squadron at Culdrose in Cornwall. On Thursday, 18 November, on his second public engagement, he switched on the Christmas lights in London's Regent Street from Jaeger House.

On 11 June 1984, Andrew arrived by Lynx helicopter on board the frigate HMS *Brazen*, his posting now for nearly two years. Six months later he set sail in her for the Falklands, to relieve (with another frigate) three ships patrolling the seas. On 11 May 1985, now bearded, he was at San Carlos with the Governor, Sir Rex Hunt, for the unveiling of a memorial to those who died in the landings there. After laying a wreath in the hillside cemetery overlooking the strait once known as Bomb Alley, Andrew said: "It's a strange sensation in some ways. But a fulfillment in another," adding that returning after three years was like a pilgrimage. The next day, he was one of the many islanders and construction-workers attending the official opening, in a huge new hanger, of the new airfield at Mount Pleasant, near Port Stanley. HMS *Brazen*, on her way back to England, docked at Baltimore in Maryland on 2 June. Hundreds of girls were at the quayside. But press attempts to photograph Andrew with female company were strongly dealt with. It was on his return, that, during Royal Ascot week, he had lunch with Sarah Ferguson.

On 14 June 1985, after a Service of Thanksgiving in St Paul's Cathedral, Andrew laid a wreath before a memorial in the crypt, unveiled by the Queen, to the 255 servicemen who were killed during the Falklands Campaign (*left*). The following week he flew off to Canada on an 8-day tour of New Brunswick and Nova Scotia, and found time to visit his old school, Lakefield. Back in England in July, he went on a pilot's continuation training course at HMS *Osprey* in Portland, Dorset, before returning to his ship, HMS *Brazen*. Not much has been said about his time on *Brazen*. But a Petty Officer cook later revealed: 'Most officers have a glass of wine with their meal. But not him. His drink was tomato juice and Worcester sauce. Even toasting the Queen he would have the minutest drop in the bottom of his glass, and dilute that with water. He didn't like rich food. His real favourite was hamburger and chips.'

In 1982 Andrew holidayed in the West Indies, on the island of Mustique. Among his guests in Princess Margaret's house were Koo Stark, and her mother. Kathleen Dee-Anne Stark, called Koo, was three years older than Andrew, and the daughter of Wilbur Stark, an American film producer. Small, slim and intensely attractive, she had met Andrew in Tramps in February 1982, after she had broken off her engagement to a millionaire advertising executive, Robert Winsor. An actress, she had appeared semi-nude in *The Americanisation of Emily*, a film produced by the Earl of Pembroke (fourth cousin of both the Princess of Wales and Sarah Ferguson). Koo had often written to Andrew during the Falklands campaign. They flew out to Mustique as Mr and Mrs Cambridge. The press now had a field day, and even led Prince Edward to complain later about their conduct. 'He was only a sailor. He'd been at war. He wanted to get away from everything and relax, unwind and get some sun ... Not only did they hound him over the affair, they actually hounded him to the extent that he had to stop the holiday. He came back from that holiday more drawn, more tired, than he had from three months at war.' This was on 13 October. Back at Culdrose – no longer a co-pilot but 'captain' of a Sea-King – he was pursued by the press and ribbed by his fellow officers. But he continued to see Koo Stark, enchanted by her.

In January 1983, Andrew returned to HMS *Invincible*. The carrier took part in a NATO exercise before sailing on 31 January to the West Indies and Florida on a goodwill tour. Koo Stark happened to be in Florida, at the time of his 23rd birthday. On shore-leave in the Bahamas and in Barbados there were rumours of parties involving other girls. But there was much work to do. The tour took in Belize and Gibraltar, the carrier returning to port on 28 April. On 19 September, Andrew began his advanced training on Lynx helicopters with 702 Naval Air Squadron at Portland in Dorset. By then, his affair with Koo Stark was over. Although she had stayed at Balmoral in August 1983, the Palace (and his father) had not approved: she was an American and had acted in a soft-porn film. In August 1984, Koo married the Green Shield heir, Tim Jefferies, another younger man. But they separated 18 months later. Meanwhile, Andrew acquired a succession of pretty girl-friends, models and actresses, including the Hon Carolyn Herbert (daughter of Lord Porchester, the Queen's racing manager), Clare Park, Katie Rabett, Finola Hughes, and Leslie Ash.

Katie Rabett was introduced to Prince Andrew at the Hamilton Gallery, Mayfair, in November 1983, when some of his photographs were being exhibited with those of seven other amateur photographers (including Koo Stark and a taxi-driver) in 'Personal Points of View.' The exhibition was the idea of an ex-American GI of Filipino descent, Gene Nocon, who was to become Andrew's technical assistant and printer. The home of Katie Rabett's parents became a focus of press attention in February 1984 – he celebrated his birthday there – and she featured (photographed in and beside a lake in Windsor Great Park) in his book, *Photographs*. In June 1986, Katie married Kit Hesketh-Harvey, the ex-Etonian half of a two-man cabaret duo 'Kit and the Widow'. Andrew was promoted to full Lieutenant on his 24th birthday, which he celebrated with Katie Rabett and others on 19 February 1984. His salary rose from £170 a week to £200.

David Frost had asked him on TV-am in November 1983 if there was a theme to his photographs. He replied: 'The theme is in fact loneliness. If you look at them, as a painting, there's not much *there* – there's nobody in them. There's maybe only one man, a person walking towards me. He's not involved with me – he's completely separate.' Andrew went on, jokingly: 'I'm a recluse. I try and keep out of people's way. I try to avoid the press ... I find that taking pictures of the family is great fun. But they do get slightly annoyed and complain bitterly that I'm behaving more and more like a pressman.' Being in the Navy and being a Prince were, he added, two completely different life-styles, and reconciling them was sometimes difficult. 'It's like being a conscious schizophrenic. Sometimes I laugh at it ...'

Photography was now taking up much of his spare time. Andrew bought his first camera after *Invincible* returned from the Caribbean to England in 1983. The following year, using the studio workshop of Gene Nocon in Covent Garden, he took the pictures for the 1985 Ilford Calendar, previewed in September 1984; and in September 1985, he not only took the official first birthday photos of Prince Harry (which were duly criticised for their amateurishness), but also had a book of his photographs published on 30 September, called *Photographs*. By now he had set up a darkroom in the Palace, converted from an old bathroom, and had at least five Nikon cameras. Early in 1986 he took the official photos of his mother and father on the occasion of her 60th birthday.

Katie Rabett

Koo Stark

Prince Andrew (*left*) launches *Photographs*. Clay-pigeon shooting (*below left*) is one of his favourite pastimes.

Finola Hughes and Clare Park

41

(*Top left*) Ronald as a baby. (*Top centre*) Five miniatures of the Ferguson family; *top*: Emily born 1841, *centre*: John born 1834 and his wife Sophia. *Below*: A. H. born 1899 and his wife Marian. Red hair runs in the family. (*Top right*) Ronald, aged 7, as a page at a wedding. (*Centre*) Major A. H. Ferguson leads the Sovereign's Escort in May 1935 – George V's and Queen Mary's Silver Jubilee. (*Below left*) at Eton aged 13. (*Below centre*) Ronald's marriage to Susan Wright. (*Below right*) at Bembridge, Isle of Wight.

THE BRIDE

Sarah's father, Ronald Ivor Ferguson, from whom she inherited her red hair, was born in London on 10 October 1931. In August 1949 he joined the Life Guards, like his father and grandfather. He served in BAOR, Aden and Cyprus, and became a Major and Commander of the Sovereign's Escort of the Household Cavalry. He is now Prince Charles' polo manager and deputy chairman of the Guards Polo Club at Windsor Great Park. He has been playing polo for 32 years. On 17 January 1956, when he was a Lieutenant, he married Susan Mary Wright, then aged 19, at St Margaret's, Westminster. She was the youngest daughter of Fitzherbert Wright (formerly 15th/19th Hussars) of Grantham and the Hon Doreen Julia Wingfield, daughter of the 8th Viscount Powerscourt, of Enniskerry, Co Wicklow. Major Ferguson's great-grandfather, Captain John Ferguson, transferred to the Life Guards after serving with the Dragoon Guards in the Crimean War (1854–56) at Balaclava and Sebastopol.

(*Below*) Sarah on her father's lap.

(*Top left*) with Trevor Howard as military adviser on *The Charge of the Light Brigade*. (*Top right*) On honeymoon at Kitzbühel. (*Centre left*) The Queen visits the Household Cavalry Regiment, Wellington Barracks, 1967. (*Centre right*) Painting of Major Ferguson. (*Below*) Deputy Chairman of the Guards Polo Club, Windsor Great Park.

Sarah Margaret Ferguson was born in a London nursing-home, at 27 Welbeck St, on 15 October 1959. She was the second child of Major and Mrs Ferguson. The first, Jane, was born in August 1957. In 1959 the family were living in a house called Lowood, in Sunninghill, near Ascot in Berkshire, a few miles south of Windsor. Major Ferguson was then a Captain in the Life Guards. He retired, as a major, in 1968 and became Prince Charles' polo manager in 1972. Sarah went to a local kindergarten, Mrs Latham's, at Englefield Green, and when she was 3 sat on her first pony, encouraged by her mother, an excellent horsewoman, who would later remark, of Sarah's first childhood meeting with Andrew: 'My recollection – I think the first time that I can remember – was that it was on the polo ground, the usual place where everybody meets.'

Sarah's elder sister, Jane Louisa, was born in London on 26 August 1957. She married an Australian grazier, wheatfarmer and polo player, William Alexander Makim, on 20 July 1976, in All Saints Church, Dummer. They have a son, Seamus Alexander aged 5, and a baby girl, Ayesha Louisa, born on 22 January 1986. Alex Makim, now 35, runs an 8,000-acre spread in northern New South Wales, near the Queensland border.

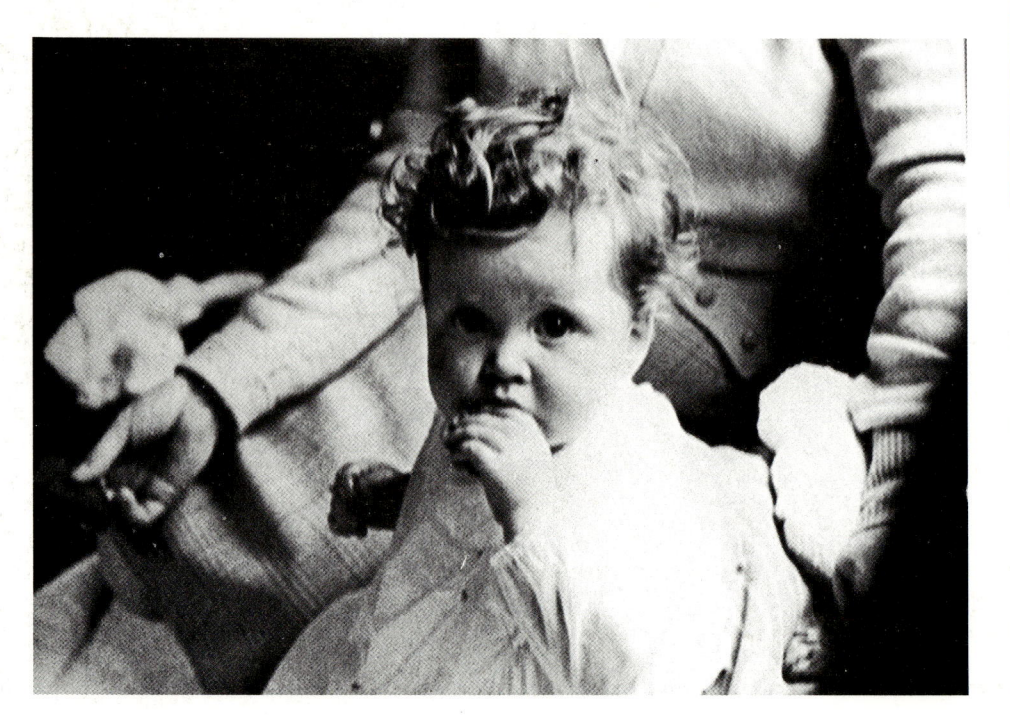

Sarah, aged 2, in September 1961 at Littlestone-on-Sea, Kent (*above*).

Sarah at the wedding of her sister Jane (*top left*) in July 1976 aged 16¾, with her mother, now Mrs Hector Barrantes, and her father four months before he remarried.

Baby Sarah (*left and right*).

Lowood (*right, inset*).

45

Holidays were spent at holiday resorts on the Sussex and Somerset coasts, and in Cornwall.

Sarah's first pony was a Shetland called Nigger, but she always had a special affection for Peanut (*top left*), the family pony. Her favourite pet was a Pekinese called Solly.

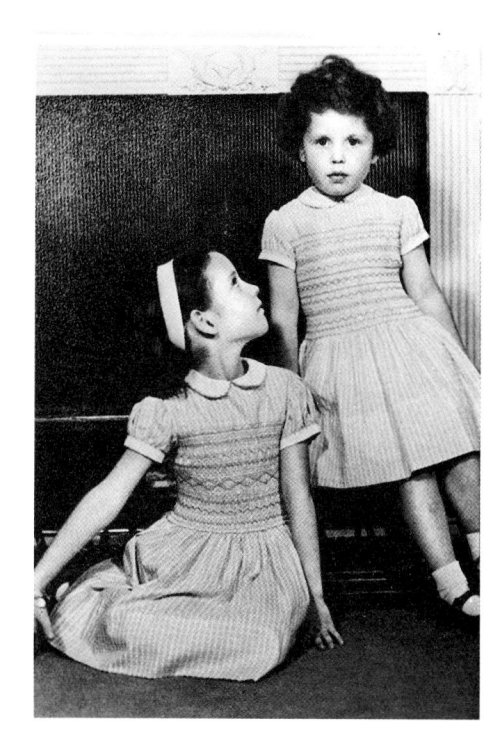

Sarah's nanny, Ritva Risu, from Finland, joined the Ferguson family when she was 22; 'Sarah and Jane never gave much trouble,' she said later. 'They got on very well. They quarrelled over toys (her favourite was Mr Rabbit (*right*)) and Sarah would cry. But usually she got her own way. She was just so full of energy. Jane was more lady-like, while Sarah was more of a tomboy . . . I always took Sarah and Jane along to watch her father play polo at Windsor. It was there I met the Royals.' And it was there that Andrew and Sarah met, most casually, amongst a crowd of other children romping on the grass of Windsor Great Park. Said Ritva : 'They mixed together very well.' That was 23 years ago.

(*Far left*) Sarah and Jane, aged 7 and 9.

(*Left*) Sarah at Goodwood, aged 9, 1968.

(*Above*) Jane and Sarah, Christmas 1963. Sarah is aged 4.

In September 1970, when Sarah (*back row centre*) was nearly 11, she went to Daneshill House, a boarding-school in Basingstoke, Hampshire, which Jane Vallance had opened with her sister Eleanor in 1950. Miss Vallance recalled a day when Sarah badly gashed her knee. 'Little Sarah – she was a rather frail child at that time – fell out of a top bunk bed. She was rascalling around, like most of the girls do. I took her to hospital and she bled all over the back seat of my car. But she never complained – she never moaned or whined . . . I think this Prince Andrew is a pretty lucky chap. And I think if he plays around a bit any more, he'll get a jolly good slap from an old Daneshill girl.' Sarah left in July 1972. Daneshill is now a day preparatory school, and two of Major Ferguson's other children, Andrew and Alice, go there now.

In 1968 when Sarah was eight, the family moved into Dummer Down Farm (*above*) in Hampshire after the death of Colonel A. H. Ferguson.

As a child and teenager Sarah was average at most games and sports: rounders, swimming, diving, tennis, and horse-riding. According to a friend: 'She rode very hard and fast in junior competitions, gymkhanas and pony club hunter trials. She loved the rough and tumble and had plenty of guts.' She won several rosettes. But at skiing she was better than most. Her father said: 'Mind you, she should have been quite good. She started when she was four, and each year we went to Austria or Switzerland.' He added: 'She was always very cheerful and full of fun . . . She's a very kind girl, a very sweet girl. But she has a lot of common sense.'

Sarah, aged 9, at Verbier in March 1963 (*above right and far right*).

Jane with Sarah, aged 13, at the time when their mother left home, 1973 (*right*).

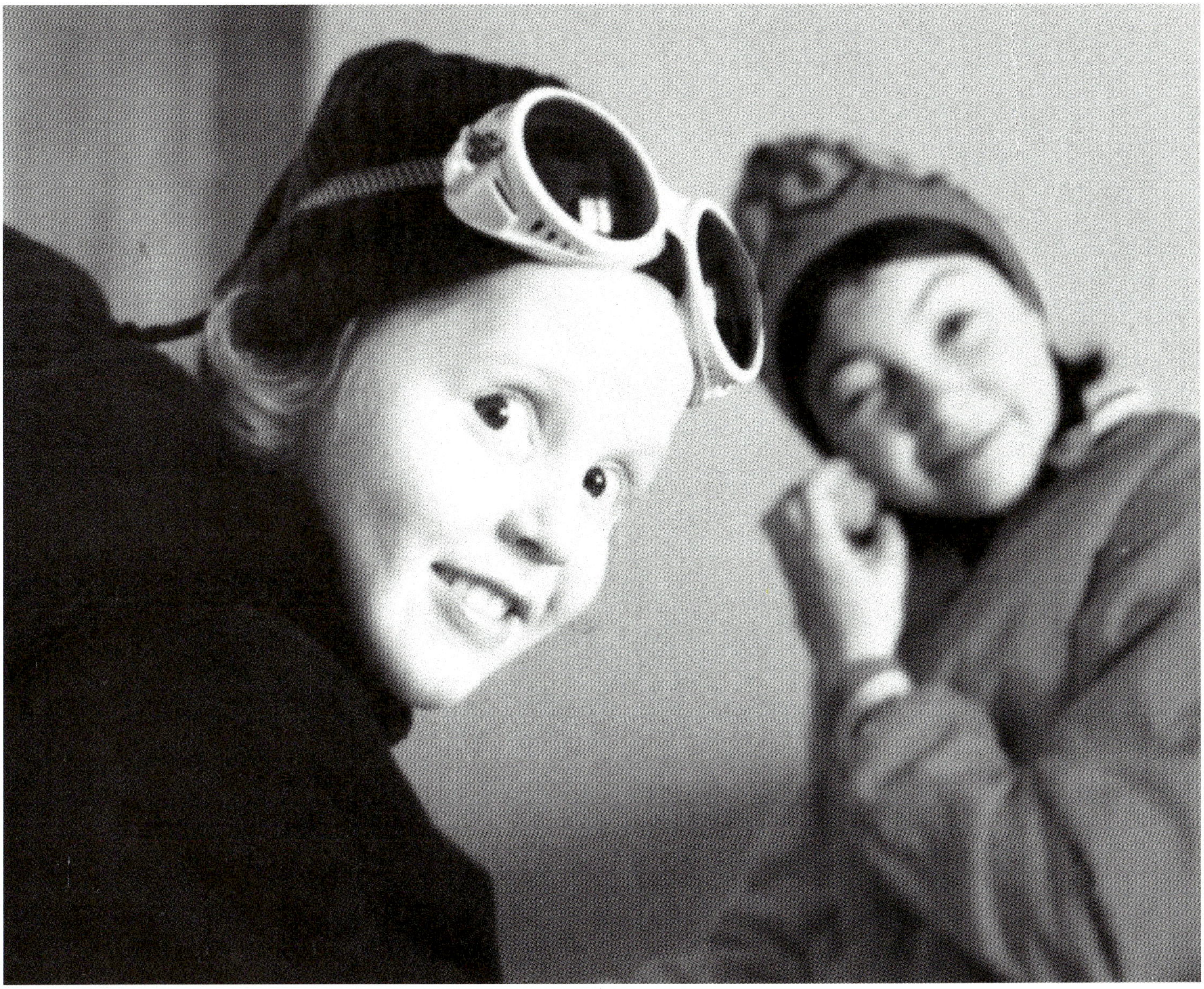

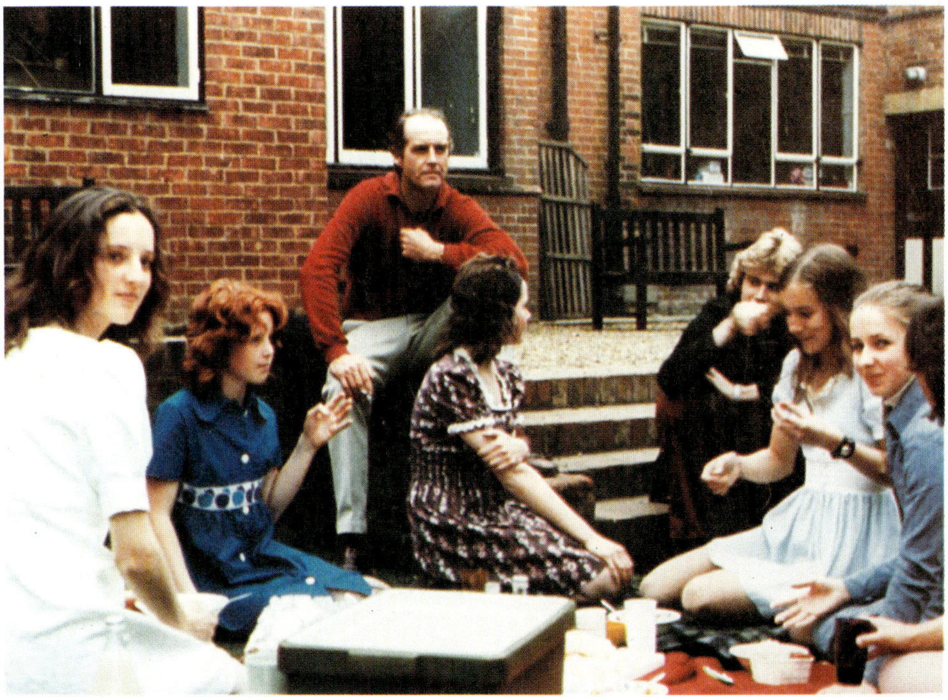

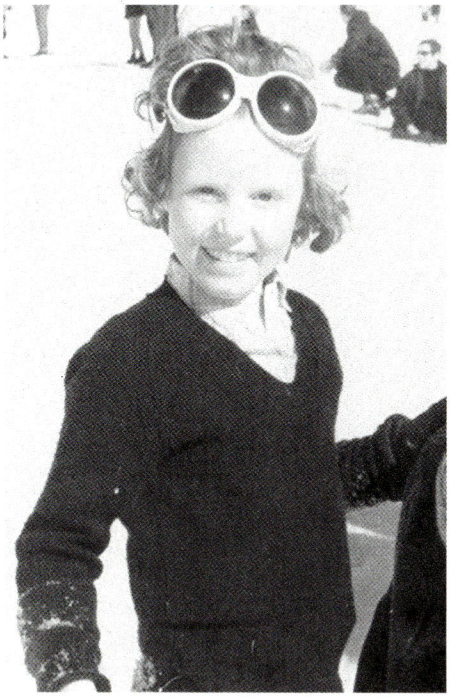

After Daneshill, Sarah followed her sister Jane as a boarder to Hurst Lodge (*below left*) Day and Boarding School for Girls in Sunningdale, near Ascot (£1,335 a term). She went there in September 1972, a few weeks before her 14th birthday. Sarah's parents were divorced in April 1974, her mother remarrying later that year. Sarah was bewildered by her mother's departure, and became even more attached to her father. But there was no resentment. Her resilience surprised some people. 'We were aware of the divorce, because we were told,' said Jo Smale, her art teacher at Hurst Lodge. 'But we wouldn't have known from Sarah. She seemed to adjust very well to the situation.'

(*Above left*) Major and Mrs Ferguson, Jane and Sarah, at Lowood in 1968. Sarah is 8, the year they left to live at Dummer.

(*Below*) Sarah, aged 18, in Cornwall.

Sarah was 16 in October 1975, soon after the start of her last year at Hurst Lodge. She became Captain of Netball and was joint Head Girl with Fenella Rodgers, daughter of comedian, Ted Rodgers (she married in 1981). Fenella was head of the day-girls, and Sarah of the boarders. She told her father she had been chosen because she was uncontrollable and would 'have to start behaving.' The headmistress, Celia Merrick, later explained: 'We had a democratic process of girls and staff electing the Head Girls. Good manners were a requisite, as well as care and concern for other people. Sarah had all this.' She added: 'There was not a vestige of snobbery or side about her. She was a thoroughly outgoing girl, very warm, friendly and popular... The scholarly pursuits were not her favourite ones. She tolerated them cheerfully. But she was particularly good at art.' Mrs Merrick taught Sarah history, and in due course she took 'O' levels in Art, English Language and Literature, French and Biology, and CSEs in Geography and Maths. She left Hurst Lodge in July 1976.

Other girls at Hurst Lodge in 1976 were: Lisa Mulidore, daughter of actress Aimi MacDonald, who went on to drama school and became an actress (appearing nude in *The Wicked Lady*); Alexandra Grant-Adamson, daughter of *The Daily Telegraph*'s diplomatic correspondent and now a staff nurse at an Ascot hospital; Jane Fransen, who now works for the House of Fraser; Davida Smart, now married, grand-daughter of Billy Smart, the circus-owner; Kerry Chippendall-Higgin, also now married and Deb of the Year in 1977; and Florence Belmondo, daughter of the French film actor, Jean-Paul Belmondo. Lisa, Alex, Jane, and Davida said of Fergie – 'On school open days, I always remember Fergie surrounded by younger pupils. They hero-worshipped her' – 'We were all terribly bored in maths one day. Everyone began throwing pencils, paper and rubbers out of the window. Fergie was very boisterous' – 'There were four of us in the dormitory. We spent most of our time talking about things at school' – 'Fergie always got things done. Not by ordering people about but because she inspired loyalty.'

On 19 November 1976, Major Ferguson remarried, his second wife being Susan Rosemary Deptford. They have three children: Andrew Frederick John, who was born in September 1978, Alice Victoria aged 5, and Eliza Charlotte, born 9 October 1985. One of her godfathers was Prince Charles.

(*Below*) Susan Ferguson on her wedding day.

Susan Ferguson, aged 39, is the daughter of a Norfolk farmer, Frederick Deptford, and a former debutante. She was brought up on her father's 1,500 acre farm at Emneth, near Wisbech. She went to school at Riddlesworth Hall in Norfolk and at Queenswood in Hertfordshire. After studying French at the Sorbonne in Paris, where she also learned about French cuisine, she and a good friend, Angela Hill, cooked for motor millionaire Timothy Rootes at his villa on the Costa Smeralda in Sardinia. Two years later they opened their own restaurant called Rosemary's – Angela's second name was also Rosemary. After that Susan Deptford cooked directors' lunches in the City of London for the Bank of America. She first met Major Ronald Ferguson at a cocktail party in London in 1974. Sarah was just seventeen when her father remarried, but although she was very close to her mother, she went out of her way to make her stepmother feel welcome. 'She was enthusiastic about me becoming part of the family,' said Susan Ferguson. 'The wicked stepmother bit is just a joke. She did it to tease me. Actually, I don't know how I would have coped if *she* hadn't. As it is, we're very good friends. I don't feel like her stepmother at all. We get on like a couple of girl-friends, as any girl-friends would.'

Susan with Bella.

On 24 January 1977, Sarah began a basic 9-month course at Queen's Secretarial College. Here she met Charlotte Eden, daughter of Lord John Eden, and now married to the Hon Mungo McGowan, youngest brother of the 3rd Baron McGowan. They have an 850-acre estate at Braunston in Northamptonshire, about 8 miles west of Althorp. 'We were at the College,' said Charlotte, 'because we knew it was important to get some sort of training, and we both managed to scrape through our courses. Money was very tight. Fergie was much more likely to be rushing to a corner café for a take-away hamburger than sipping champagne.' When the course ended on the 16 December 1977, the girls remained friends, and in 1980 Sarah got Charlie a job at her place of work, Durden-Smith Communications. At the end of that year both girls flew to Argentina to spend Christmas with Sarah's mother and stepfather at Tres Lomas. Sarah was now 21. They then set out for America, travelling north through South America, into Mexico, on to Florida, then Washington and New York. It took them four months. 'We travelled by bus to start with,' said Charlotte. 'It was pretty rough. The roads were bumpy and the buses were old, we shared them with farmers and chickens. We had a guidebook and used it to find all the cheapie places to sleep.' On the Argentine border they ran out of money. 'There weren't any banks and so we slept in the bus station on benches. Slept isn't quite the word. It was a great adventure.'

(*Left*) Sarah in the Argentine, aged 21.
(*Below*) Skiing with Charlotte McGowan.

Sarah's first job was as an interviewer with Flatmates Unlimited, a flat-sharing agency in Brompton Road, Earls Court. Her boss at the time, Wendy Keith, said later that she was 'helpful, bubbly, intelligent and a great people person.' She now had a car, a VW Golf, and was constantly zipping between town and country, involved in the social whirl of dinners, wine-bars and shows, and weekends with friends. She also went to Switzerland at least twice a year. In December 1978, she became an executive secretary with a public relations firm, Durden-Smith Communications, in Knightsbridge. A colleague said: 'She was permanently on the phone. But that's what happens when you employ someone like that with good social connections.' Her boss, however (Neil Durden-Smith, married to TV presenter, Judith Chalmers) said: 'She was a great girl, a one-hundred-per-center.' She was there for 2½ years. After that, she worked for an art dealer, William Drummond, and was a temp for several months, working more than once for Durden-Smith's new company, Sports Sponsorship International. She shared a flat in Prince of Wales Terrace in W8.

(*Below*) Sarah at her eighteenth birthday party in the Berkeley Hotel.

In July 1979, Lady Diana Spencer, then just 18, and three other girls took over a flat in Coleherne Court, off the Old Brompton Road. Two months later she began working at the Young England Kindergarten in Pimlico. It was about this time that she and Sarah Ferguson met, a casual acquaintance at first that blossomed into a friendship after Diana's marriage in 1981, when the girls began meeting at polo grounds, where Sarah's father, Major Ferguson, was overseeing Prince Charles' polo ponies and games.

Sarah, with her hair in a plait, photographed with her mother and the Prince and Princess of Wales at Windsor Great Park (*above*) long before there was any thought in Sarah's mind of herself one day becoming a princess.

In 1980, Sarah began associating with an old Etonian, Kim Smith-Bingham (*far right above*), three years older than her. As with Paddy McNally (*far right below*) later, and Prince Andrew, she had known of him and was friendly with him several years before any romance began. Smith-Bingham's sister, Laura, who works in a superior gift-shop, Present Affairs, in Fulham Road, was and is a close friend. She is now married to a wine merchant, John Goedhuis. Sarah first met Smith-Bingham in Argentina, where he was working on a ranch for six months after leaving Eton. She was 17. He saw very little of her then. But three years later, in 1980, they met up again in London and began going out together.

'We never lived together,' he told the *Daily Mail*. 'But we did spend a lot of time with each other. I was working in Verbier in Switzerland, selling ski clothes and equipment, and she'd come over, perhaps for a month; and in the summer I'd spend time in England to be with her and of course my family.' He spent weekends at Dummer, but usually they went off to stay with friends. They joked about the fact that he also had a stepmother. In Verbier, where there was a large, international crowd of people, Sarah would ski every day while he was working. 'She's very good', he said. 'Black run standard.' In the evening they would go out to restaurants and see friends, having fun on sleigh-rides and fondu parties. But they were not thought of as a long-term couple. Their names weren't written on the same dinner party invitation; they were invited separately. After three years they split up. 'It was simply a question of each starting to live a different life-style,' he said. In 1984, he married Fiona Macdonald-Buchanan, aged 30, daughter of Major Sir Reginald Narcissus Macdonald-Buchanan of the Scots Guards. Her previous marriage, to Nigel Pilkington, was dissolved after 8 years in 1983. The Smith-Binghams have a baby daughter, Marina. They returned to England in 1985, and he set up a business, Offshore Sports. 'We still see Fergie,' he said. 'We're in the same set after all and still good friends. But when we meet now we keep our chat pretty light-hearted.'

On the bonnet of Sarah's blue BMW 318 is a mascot, a silver owl. It was given to her by her first steady boy-friend Kim Smith-Bingham, and not by Prince Andrew. Prince Charles exchanged similar gifts with his future bride, Lady Diana. He gave her a diving silver frog, and she presented him with a polo pony and rider. Smith-Bingham originally acquired the owl mascot when he drove a car with an OWL registration number.

Paddy McNally, now 48, is a motor-racing consultant and used to manage Grand Prix champion, Nikki Lauda. After his wife died of cancer in 1983, Sarah, who had known him for several years, used to visit his homes in Geneva and in Verbier, and looked after his two young sons, Sean and Rollo, now 16 and 13 and at a Roman Catholic boarding school, Stonyhurst. 'Of course we were very close,' said McNally later. He denied that Sarah had given him an ultimatum about marrying her. 'My parting from Sarah was very amicable. It was an adult situation and there was absolutely no jealousy attached. We're still very good friends.' He went on: 'Sarah is very much her own woman. She will go far, very far. She's a girl in a million. Any man who is with her has a fantastic girl.'

Since the spring of 1981, Sarah Ferguson has worked as a publisher's editor for Richard Burton, SA, in the fourth floor office of BCK Graphic Arts SA, in Saint George Street, W1 (*left*), at the rear of Sotheby's. Her business card describes her as a 'Directrice'. BCK is a Swiss fine arts printing company based in Geneva. The chairman of both companies, Richard Burton, aged 47, said : 'We work 18 hours a day when necessary. When it's not, I don't mind if people disappear for the weekend. The job doesn't require a vast knowledge of art. It's more a matter of common sense, and Fergie has lots of that. She has a wonderful sense of humour, and we laugh a lot together. It's a great help when you're working under pressure.' Sarah is believed to be earning about £12,500 a year. Last year she was involved in the preparation of *The New Painting : Impressionism 1874–86*, which was published in December 1985. Then she worked on a book of Italian architectural drawings from the Queen's collection at Windsor, and most recently on *The Palaces of Westminster*, a history of their treasures, with author Sir Robert Cooke, former Conservative MP for Bristol West.

In 1983 Sarah moved into a two-bedroom ground floor flat (*right*) in Lavender Gardens, between Clapham Junction and the Common. Her landlady was Carolyn Beckwith-Smith, cousin of the Princess of Wales' chief lady-in-waiting, Anne Beckwith-Smith, aged 34 and daughter of Major Beckwith-Smith. At one time, there was a possibility that Sarah might also become a lady-in-waiting. Her flatmate, Carolyn, aged 30, ran a shopping agency in partnership with Lady Settrington, who as Sally Clayton was a member of Pan's People. Sally had married an old Etonian, Charles, Lord Settrington in 1976. In due course he will become Earl of March (when his father becomes the 10th Duke of Richmond and Gordon). Carolyn married another old Etonian, a baronet's son, Harry Cotterrell, aged 24, in July 1986. He runs a laundry and valet service in Chelsea.

Major Ferguson and his second wife, Susan, live with their three children at Dummer Down Farm, an 876-acre farm just off the M3, southwest of Basingstoke. Both the Fergusons are closely involved in community activities and charities, as well as in the working life of the farm. Susan Ferguson stripped and decorated the farmhouse attic bedrooms now used by the three children. The family have a Jack Russell terrier called Bella. She is the Major's mascot, and features as such, in silver, on the bonnet of his red BMW. Susan Ferguson drives her own and other children to school when it's her turn on the school run. She looks after her home with the help of a 'daily' and a nanny, who is married and lives out. In addition to doing the shopping and 'some of the gardening', she is actively involved with several charities, including the Youth Hostels Association, the NSPCC, and Birthright. The latter charity, founded 22 yeas ago as the Childbirth Research Centre, is devoted to the health and welfare of babies before, during and after birth. The Princess of Wales' gynaecologist, Mr George Pinker, is on its council, and the Princess is herself the charity's patron. In recent years she has opened two of Birthright's four units.

Major Ferguson's mother, Lady Elmhirst, lives in the village of Dummer. In 1953, to commemorate the Coronation, she presented the village with a wooden bus shelter (*far right*).

The christening of Eliza Ferguson in 1986 (*above right and right*). Standing beside their parents are Andrew and Alice.

Susie Ferguson left the family home in 1973, when Sarah was 13, to marry Hector Barrantes, an Argentinian landowner and polo player. They married in a register office in Buenos Aires in 1974. She met him when he was playing for the Hon Mark Vestey's team, Foxcote. Both he and Major Ferguson play polo at No 4, as a defensive back. Prince Charles, another No 4, made his high-goal debut with Foxcote in 1973. Senor Barrantes (his highest handicap was 7 – the top is 10) earns over £100,000 a year as a polo professional. He also has a ranch at Tres Lomas, some 300 miles southwest of Buenos Aires. For part of the year he and his wife live in Palm Beach, Florida, where he coaches the polo team of White Birch. Senor Barrantes' team won the Queen's Cup in June 1980, two years before the Falklands Campaign. He has not played polo in Britain since, as Argentinian polo-players were banned in 1983 by the Hurlingham Polo Association from playing in the UK.

Susie Barrantes, 49 in June 1986, said at the Palm Beach Polo and Country Club before the engagement: 'My daughter is very happy, and having a lot of fun, the most fun she has ever had. She tells me everything, because we are close, very close indeed. But it's hard for a girl as young as she is to be in the public gaze, and the last thing she wants is a mother to make that any harder. It would be wrong of me to say anything other than that my daughter is having the time of her life.'

Hector Barrantes (*above left*) after his team had won the Queen's Cup in June 1980.

Susie Barrantes (*below left*) arrives at Heathrow airport from Argentina in April 1986.

According to Kim Smith-Bingham, Sarah is a very good cook and hostess and likes giving small dinner parties. But she isn't a wine buff. And she never smokes. She likes being given chocolates and flowers – roses are her favourite – and appreciates other traditional courtesies, like men opening doors for her and paying for meals. She doesn't read much, mainly romances (Jilly Cooper's novels being tops) and at the theatre and cinema prefers the glamour and entertainment values of musicals: *Barnum, Cats, Grease, Saturday Night Fever, A Chorus Line*. She likes going to a good show and having a good meal, French, Italian, Mexican or Chinese for choice. She isn't keen on nightclubs. In TV, comedy programmes go down best with her – *Spitting Image* is a special joy. Her musical tastes, as in other matters, are like those of the Princess of Wales – nothing too heavy, Elton John and bands like Police, Dire Straits and Supertramp. When Sarah lived in Clapham, she shopped at the supermarkets, bicycling to and fro, principally to keep in trim, and drank halves of lager in a local pub. Carolyn Beckwith-Smith said of her as a lodger: 'She keeps the place clean and does most of the shopping, but she either leaves the cooking to me or we eat out.'

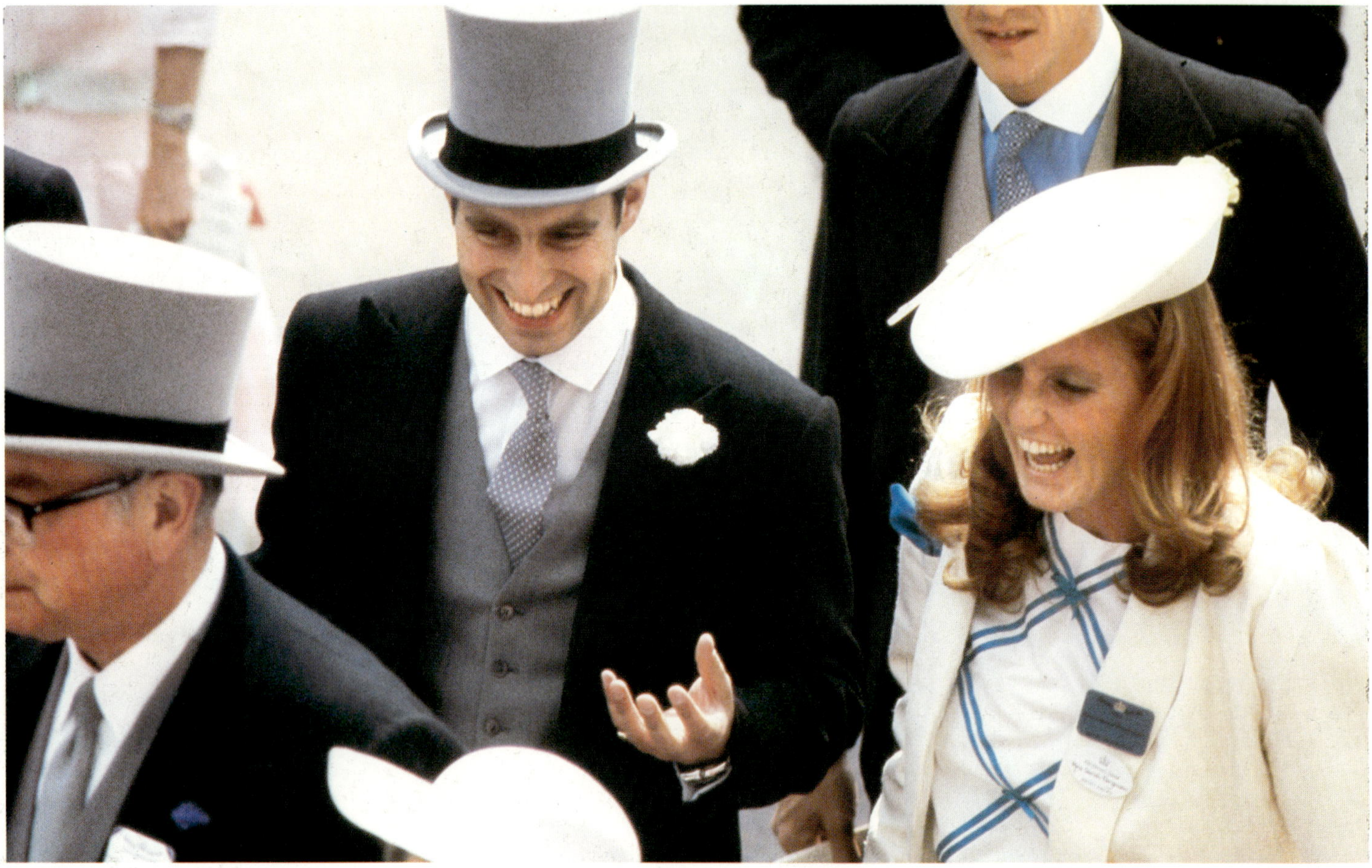

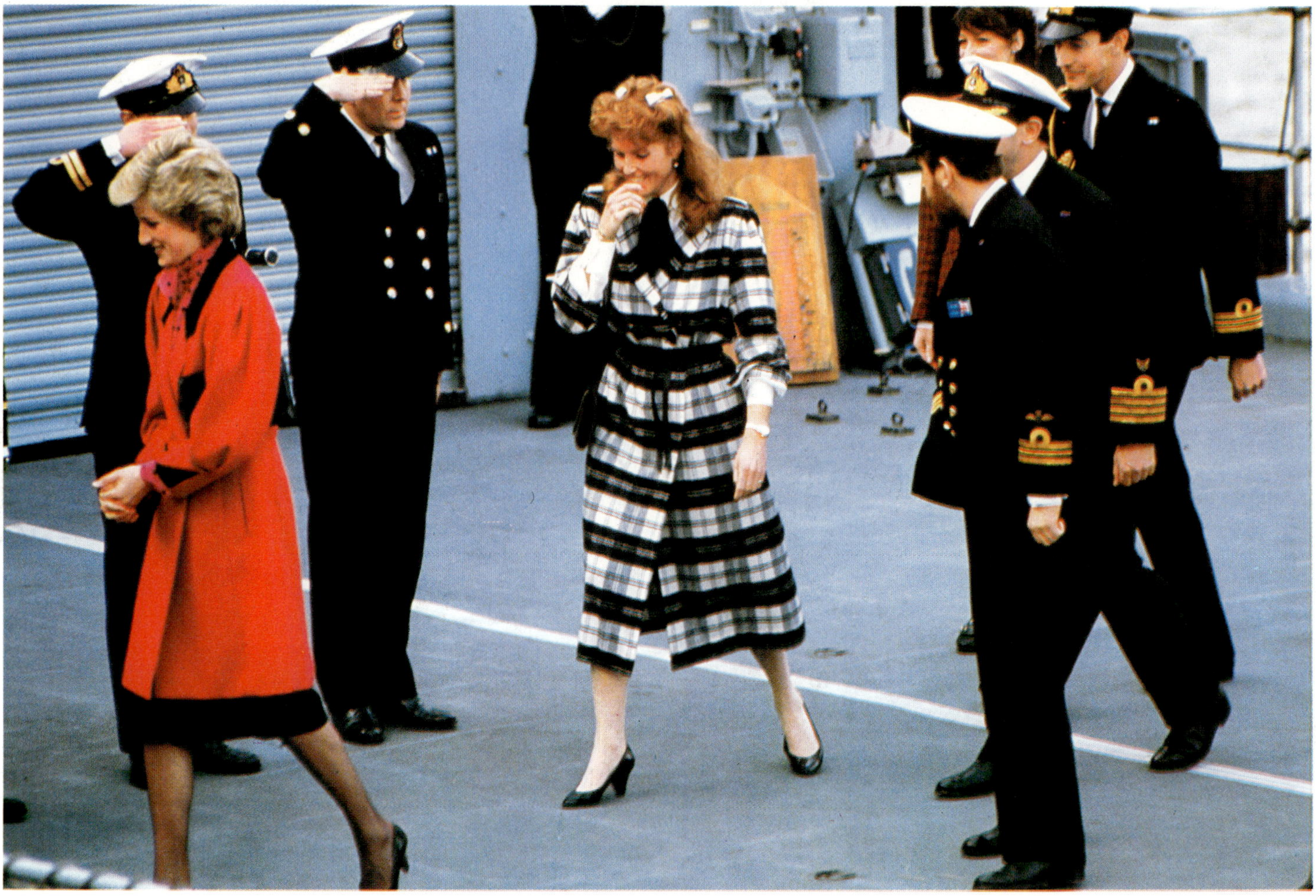

Despite Sarah's aristocratic background and life in London, she isn't a Sloane Ranger and dislikes being described as one. Nor does she dress like one – like the headscarf-wearing, tweedily-tailored upper-crust girls of Kensington and Chelsea. Her casual clothes are much more Bohemian and colourful, those of an art-lover, worn to conceal her buxom size 14 figure, as are long skirts that drape and swirl, and thick shawls, scarves and sweaters that hide her bust. She believes, it seems, that strong patterns and colours, and bright or brassy jewellery, are best for her. And trousers are out. Designers she has favoured include Alistair Blair, Phillippa Mackinnon, Gina Fratini and Paul Golding. When dressing for a social occasion she will be quite bold, accentuating all her attributes, especially her red hair, her greatest asset and much admired by Prince Andrew. Her hair is styled and conditioned by Denise McAdam of Michaeljohn, a 28-year-old Scot. Sarah, who has tried out various new styles, usually involving flowers and ribbon bows, has been criticised for wearing outfits described as 'boring, bulky and busy,' with too many bows, buttons and belts. She is no more worried about her weight than any other girl and has never been on a diet. Her hats have been made by Freddie Fox of New Bond Street, including those she wore at the Royal Wedding in 1981, at Royal Ascot in 1985 (*top left*), and on the Queen's Birthday in April 1986.

THE WEEKS BEFORE THE WEDDING

On Thursday, 20 March, Sarah left Buckingham Palace in a chauffeur-driven car to go to work, attended by uniformed and armed policemen (including Prince Andrew's personal bodyguard, Detective Inspector Geoff Padgham). Barriers lined the street, holding back a large crowd and a barrage of clicking photographers, as she arrived at BCK. Almost shyly she paused on the pavement and held up her left hand to display the engagement ring. Perhaps flustered by it all, she then tripped over the doorstep. It was 1.12 when she left, to be greeted again by crowds of pressmen, shoppers and office-workers. But within a few days she stopped coming to BCK and worked from the Palace, where she took over several rooms on the second floor, which had once been Prince Andrew's.

On Sunday, 23 March, Sarah and Andrew visited her mother's mother, the Hon Mrs Doreen Wright, of Calne in Wiltshire. On the Tuesday, the date and place of the wedding were announced – in Westminster Abbey on 23 July 1986. Calls for a national holiday on the day were turned down by the Government. At the end of that week the Lord Chamberlain announced that 'Royal emblems and images may not be used on textiles and clothing, apart from headscarves'. So Andrew and Fergie would not be seen on souvenir T-shirts – although they would on plates, vases and mugs, and appear in wax in Madame Tussaud's.

The Royal Family spent a bitterly cold Easter weekend, 28–31 March, at Windsor Castle. Sarah lunched with them on the Saturday, when there was something of a celebration. The party included the Queen Mother and Princess Margaret's grown-up children, Viscount Linley and Lady Sarah Armstrong-Jones. On the Sunday morning, as Andrew's fiancée, Sarah attended morning service with the Royal Family in St George's Chapel Windsor (*left*), her first public appearance with them. She wore a dog-tooth check suit and a black straw hat. Prince Charles' left arm was in a sling : he had accidentally hit his finger with a hammer at Highgrove. That night, another first – a puppet of Sarah appeared with one of Andrew on ITV's satirical show, *Spitting Image* (*far left*).

On the weekend of 4–6 April, Prince Andrew was at Nassau in the Bahamas, attending a charity dinner-dance arranged by some Gordonstoun friends. 150 guests paid £250 each to be there. It was noticeable that he didn't dance and drank nothing but water. He phoned Sarah several times. Sarah spent the weekend at Dummer Down Farm. She and Andrew met the Archbishop of Canterbury, Dr Runcie, on 10 April at Lambeth Palace. They talked for over an hour about the meaning of marriage, its responsibilities, and theirs to the christian faith. On 14 April, Sarah visited the College of Arms in London to inspect a coat of arms devised for her by the Garter King of Arms. That morning Andrew began an 7-week officers' course at the Royal Naval College, Greenwich (*above*). He was one of 40 students living in college bed-sitters during the week and studying defence policies, finance and man management. He was there until 6 June. After the honeymoon he will be stationed at HMS *Heron*, a shore base at Yeovilton in Somerset, where, with other helicopter pilots, he will take part in a complex weapons-training course, involving some with nuclear devices, which, at four months, will not be long enough to allow him married quarters. Billets in the mess are basic bed-sits.

The Queen's 60th birthday, happy and glorious despite the rain, was celebrated on Monday, 21 April, with a thanksgiving service in St George's Chapel, Windsor, attended by over a thousand close friends, courtiers, staff, estate workers, politicians, relatives and 44 members of the Royal Family, spanning four generations, from the Queen Mother, aged 85, to three-year-old Prince William. It was the first magnificent royal occasion to be attended by Sarah Ferguson, and in the afternoon she made an appearance with the Queen, Prince Philip and Prince Andrew on the balcony of Buckingham Palace, when over 6,000 children, assembled in the forecourt below, sang 'Happy Birthday Ma'am,' bearing a host of golden daffodils. Sixty white doves were released from a massive crown on a float. Then the Queen, Andrew and Sarah came down to meet the cheering children, and gather the armfuls of daffodils given to them, while thousands were scattered on the ground.

Later that night, the Queen and her husband walked through the piazza of Covent Garden, before attending a special birthday tribute, *Fanfare for Elizabeth*, at the Royal Opera House, televised live on ITV. Sarah wore a three-colour gown in duchess satin designed by Alastair Blair. That morning, her mother, Susan Barrantes, arrived in London from Buenos Aires to see her daughter, meet the Queen and discuss wedding arrangements. The day before Prince Andrew had lunch with his fiancée and her family at Dummer Down Farm for the first time.

On 23 April, the names of the bridesmaids and pages at the wedding were announced. There would be eight, all under the age of nine and related to either the bride or groom, except for the oldest bridesmaid, Lady Rosanagh Innes-Ker, aged 7, eldest daughter of the Duke and Duchess of Roxburghe. The others were Laura Fellowes, aged 6, eldest daughter of Robert and Lady Jane Fellowes, sister of the Princess of Wales; Alice Ferguson, aged 5, Sarah's half-sister and the eldest daughter of Major and Mrs Ferguson; and Zara Phillips, aged 4, daughter of Princess Anne and Captain Mark Phillips. The four pages were: Peter Phillips, aged 8, Zara's brother and seventh in the line of succession to the throne; Andrew Ferguson, aged 7, eldest child of Major and Mrs Ferguson; Seamus Makim, aged 5, eldest child of Sarah's elder sister, Jane Makim, and her Australian husband, Alex; and Prince William, aged 4 a month before the wedding, eldest son of the Prince and Princess of Wales. Prince Edward, Prince Andrew's younger brother, would be his supporter, or best man.

(*From left to right*) Seamus Makim, Alice and Andrew Ferguson.

Lady Rosanagh
Innes-Ker

Zara and Peter Phillips

Prince William

Laura Fellowes

Over the next two months, May–June 1986, Sarah Ferguson, usually without her fiancé (as he was on an officers' course at Greenwich), was seen at various occasions and in a variety of hairstyles and clothes: at a Dulwich Picture Gallery party with Princess Margaret; at a charity Fashion show in London on 2 May; at the Royal Windsor Horse Show on Saturday, 10 May; and out shopping at various stores. At the weekend, whenever possible, she would watch her father or Prince Charles play polo in Windsor Great Park. On the evening of 19 May, Sarah accompanied the Queen and Princess Margaret to the Chelsea Flower Show (*below*), taking the place of the Princess of Wales, who was relaxing after an exhausting tour of Canada and Japan.

On Tuesday, 27 May, Sarah boarded a British Airways flight (as Miss Watson) to Antigua. She stayed there, until Wednesday, 4 June, with her schoolfriend, Florence Belmondo (*above*), who married an American advertising executive in 1979. While she was away, the official souvenir of the Royal Wedding was published. It included official photographs by Terence Donovan, 49-year-old Londoner, and others by Prince Andrew. On Saturday, 7 June, Sarah was at a charity gala in Weymouth with Prince Andrew, their first official engagement together.

A heatwave hit London before the weekend of 13–16 June. Sarah, wearing a pig-tail, saw Boris Becker being beaten by Tim Mayotte at the Stella Artois tennis championships at Queen's Club, which Mayotte won in the Final, and on Saturday 14 June she watched the ceremony of Trooping the Colour, appearing later with the Royal Family on the Buckingham Palace balcony for the fly-past (*below*). On the Sunday night, she and Prince Charles were in Cambridge, watching Prince Edward's final appearance in a university revue.

Sarah's mother and Hector Barrantes flew in to London from Argentina on Monday 16 June. Mrs Barrantes met up with her daughter at the Guards Polo Club in Windsor Great Park, where Major Ferguson and Prince Charles were both involved in separate polo matches. Earlier, Sarah had paid a working visit to the annual Grosvenor House Antiques Fair. The following day, 17 June, the start of Royal Ascot, she accompanied Prince Andrew on the traditional carriage drive down the racecourse. Senor and Mrs Barrantes (*below*) had tea with the Queen in the Royal Box, while at Windsor, Major Ferguson, playing polo, was accidentally hit on the brow by a polo-stick. Sarah's outfits at Ascot came in for some criticism.

Sarah flew with Andrew to Bembridge on the Isle of Wight on Sunday 22 June, for the start of the Digital Schneider Trophy Air Race, which they watched from Ryde Pier. She was at Wimbledon on several occasions during the fortnight of the tournament. On 26 June, Sarah and Andrew were in Northern Ireland (*right*). It was her first visit, and a most happy and crowded one, taking in Belfast City Hospital, an RUC sports day, a garden party and dinner party at Hillsborough. Every week now they were seen in public together, at a broad mix of functions and events. On Sunday 29 June they were at Sealand near Chester, when Prince Andrew's royal team took part in a celebrity clay-pigeon shoot. He and Sarah were at the State Banquet in Buckingham Palace given for the West German President on 1 July; at the Boater Ball in Chelsea Barracks on 3 July; and in Southampton at a ship-naming ceremony the next day. On 9 July they visited the Household Cavalry Regiment at Hyde Park Barracks, and on the 11th the Royal Tournament.

Lindka Cierach, aged 34, was born in Africa in 1952, where her parents, a Polish Second World War hero and a British colonel's daughter, married. Lindka remembers watching her mother make their clothes. 'We lived a nomadic life, always on the move. It was idyllic.' When she was 8, she was sent to a Roman Catholic convent school in England, leaving when she was 18. For a time she was a secretary with *Vogue*, who advised her to go to the London College of Fashion. There she studied clothing technology and all aspects of design. Lindka then worked with the Japanese designer, Yuki, before setting up on her own when she was 26. 'My friends rallied round, and people began bringing me a variety of orders, including wedding dresses.' She now works from her home, a Victorian terraced house in Fulham Broadway; the workroom is in the attic. Nominated by *The Tatler* as the 'hottest society dressmaker of the year', her clients have included Queen Anne-Marie of Greece, the Duchess of Kent, Lady Rose Cecil, and more recently Carolyn Beckwith-Smith, Sarah Ferguson's former landlady. She said: 'I discovered Lindka when I was looking for a bridesmaid's dress some years ago. She is absolutely brilliant. You can go along with your own ideas and she will tell you what will work and what will not.' The dresses cost upwards of £2,000. 'I make what is called a *toile*,' said Lindka, 'a kind of dummy dress out of calico. After the *toile* I make a pattern, and then plan the bodice and the beading... The silhouette is the most important part of the whole creation. You use fashion to suit your client.'

Sarah's elder sister, Jane, 29 in August, arrived in England on Friday, 4 July, with her husband Alex Makim, their son Seamus, aged 5, and daughter, Ayesha, born in January. They stayed at Dummer Down Farm where, that night, Major and Mrs Ferguson gave an al fresco party, attended by Sarah and Prince Andrew, for over 100 villagers, local friends and estate workers. A garden party was held at the Farm on the Sunday in aid of an appeal for a baby scanner at Basingstoke Hospital; there was a band, a Welsh choir, Scottish country dancing, tea and strawberries. Susan Ferguson and Jane Makim were presented with cheques for the appeal totalling over £4,000. Then, on Tuesday, 8 July, Ayesha was christened at a private ceremony at the parish church in Dummer – 'a very special child' to her mother who suffered two miscarriages before Ayesha was born. She was named after the Maharini of Jaipur. One of her godmothers was Sarah, whose mother, father and stepmother attended the christening. Jane Makim, who was married in Dummer Church a month before her 19th birthday, celebrated her 10th wedding anniversary three days before Sarah's wedding.

Sarah's and Andrew's horoscope

Sarah is five months older than Prince Andrew. A Libran, she was born on 15 October 1959, he on the cusp of Aquarius and Pisces, on 19 February 1960. Her moon is in Aries, his in Scorpio. According to some astrologers, they are not ideally suited as partners in marriage – Andrew, it seems, is 'a rogue male' and his urge for conquest, as with Edward VII, may be difficult to contain. Some suggest that, like Princess Margaret, he has sacrificed his true feelings out of a sense of duty, and to please his mother, to whom he is devoted. They claim he may eventually rebel, if constrained too much, and become sensationally involved, like the Duke of Windsor, with a foreign woman, someone he has already briefly met. Sarah and Andrew, it seems, are passionate strangers, much enamoured of each other, and marriage now, but with little in common. According to the stars, she is sociable, kind and caring, a great hostess. He is loving but unpredictable, becoming frustrated by sub-conscious desires and dreams. He is more complex and sensitive than Sarah, more stubborn and illogical. But her practicality, her capacity for argument, persuasion and ultimate generosity should make the partnership work.

According to the Chinese horoscopes, Sarah and Andrew are more compatible married than as friends – although they should have avoided marrying in the Year of the Tiger (1986–87), a time of revolution and change. She is a Pig, and he is a Rat – as are Prince Charles, the Queen Mother, Mark Phillips and Princess Alexandra.

Sarah's and Andrew's last official appearance together before the wedding was at the Royal Tournament on the afternoon of 11 July. That night she joined the Royal Family at a glittering ball at Claridge's, given by the exiled King Constantine of Greece to celebrate the 21st birthday of his eldest daughter and the christening of his youngest son. Three days earlier Sarah had attended the christening of her sister's baby daughter, Ayesha; and on 5 July she and Andrew were guests at the wedding of her friend and former flatmate, Carolyn Beckwith-Smith, in Horsham. On the night of Prince Andrew's stag-party, held at Aubrey House in Kensington on 15 July and attended by several naval friends and by Prince Charles, (Prince Edward was in New Zealand), Elton John, David Frost, and Scottish comedian Billy Connolly, the latter's girl-friend, comedy actress Pamela Stephenson, together with the Princess of Wales, Sarah and her close friend Julie Dodd-Noble, dressed up as policewomen. Their plan was to gatecrash Andrew's dinner-jacketed party and 'arrest' him. They were advised not to do so, as press photographers, having discovered the secret venue of Andrew's party, were outside the house. The girls decided to invade a night-club, Annabel's, instead, where they remained for 15 minutes, wearing hired uniforms, wigs and glasses, and were mistaken for kissogram girls. The next morning, there was a long, tiring rehearsal at the Abbey, involving Sarah and Andrew, the eight bridesmaids and pages. This was followed by a family lunch for the couple with Mrs Barrantes and the Makims at Harry's Bar in Mayfair, and a dinner given by Prince Charles at a French restaurant in Charlotte Street. Susan Barrantes was now partnered by her husband, Hector, who had been away playing polo in the USA. Sarah and Diana then paid a return visit to Annabel's, this time with their Princes. There were other rehearsals, other celebrations, including Sarah's last public appearance at Dummer as a commoner and a single woman. Squired by Prince Andrew, she opened the church fête on Saturday, 19 July (*below*). But such was the close interest of the crowds that they left early. After attending morning service with the Queen in St George's Chapel, Windsor, on the Sunday, the couple were the guests of honour on Monday night at a lavish ball given by Major Ferguson in a giant marquee at the Guards Polo Club. It was attended by 600 guests, including many members of the Royal Family, Mrs Nancy Reagan, and show business friends, who danced until dawn, undeterred by the rain.

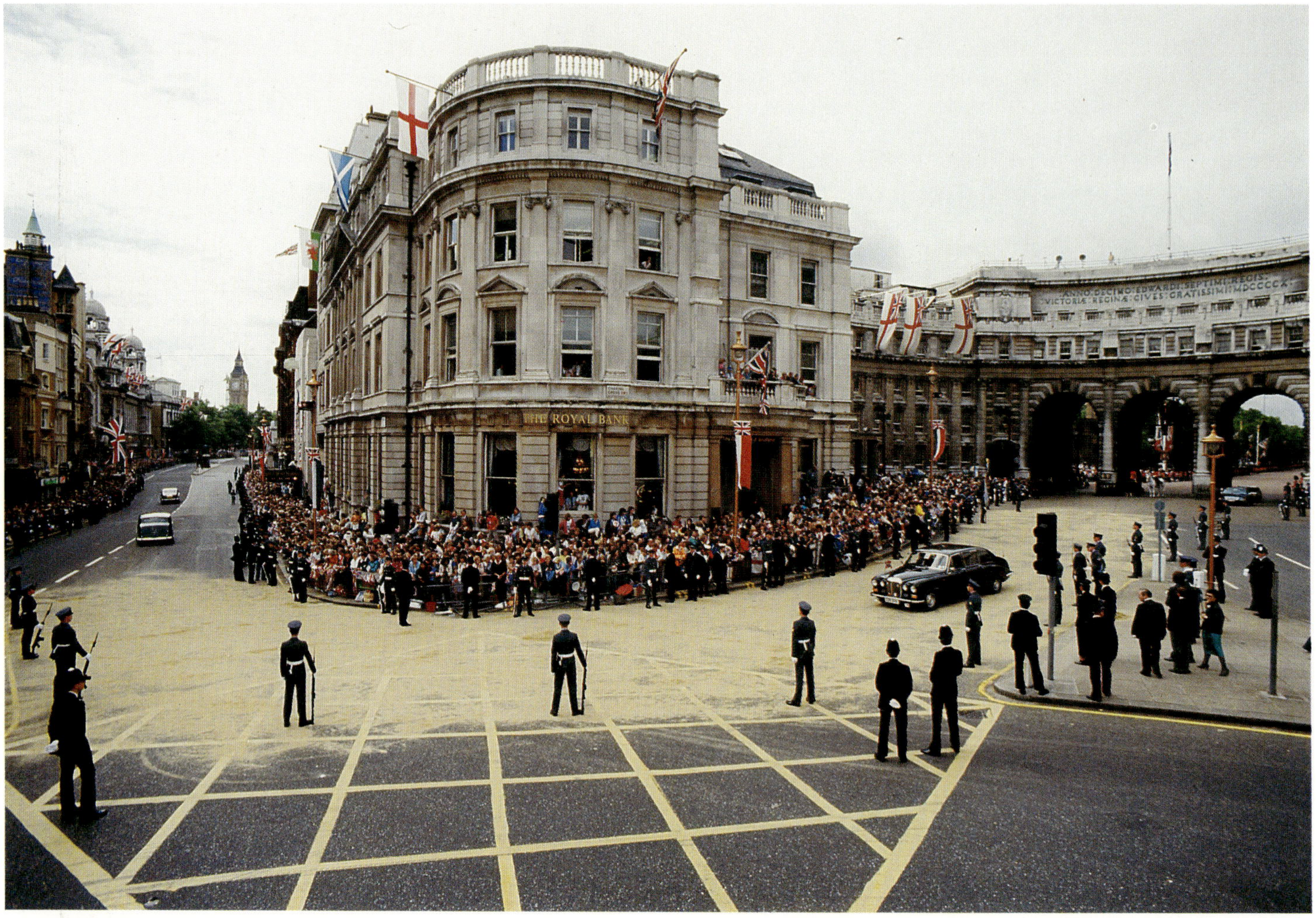
THE ROYAL BANK

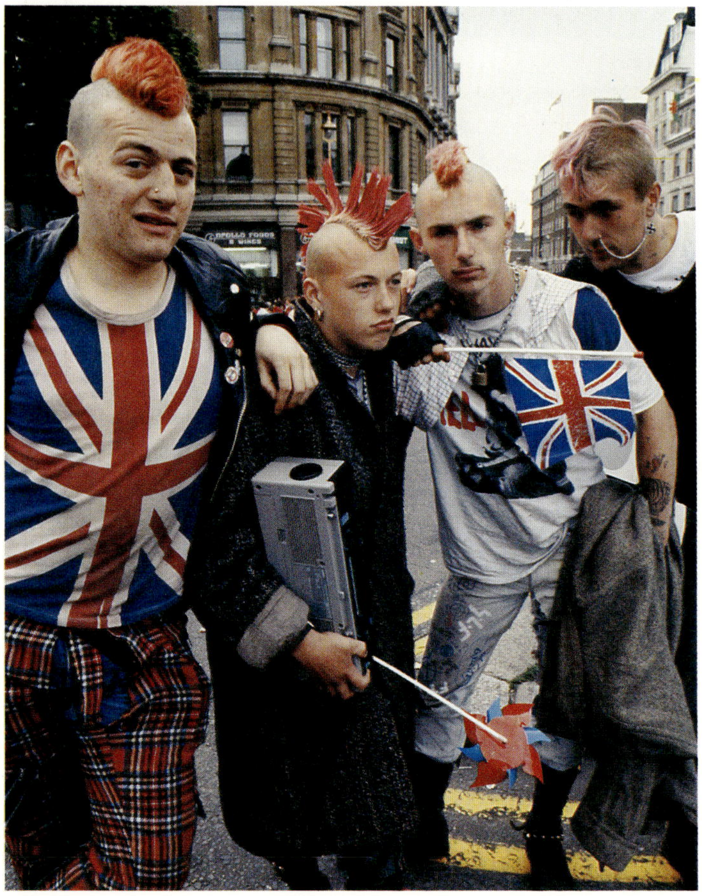

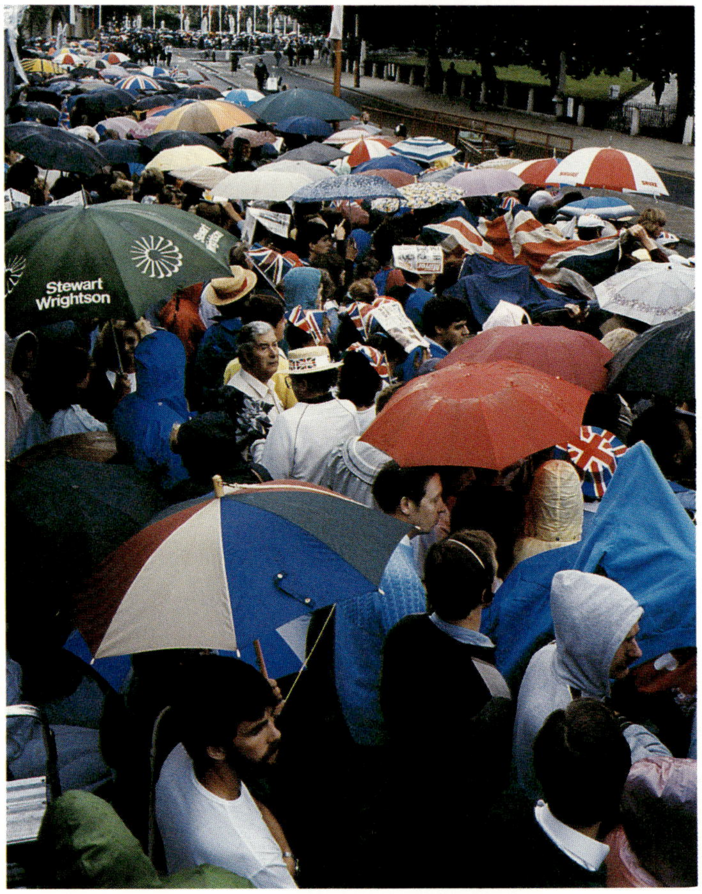
Stewart
Wrightson

THE WEDDING

THE DAY was bright and fair. The dawn was cool and still. The sun rose at 5.10 am into a citron sky awash with drifts of slate-coloured clouds. The official weather forecast for the London area said: 'Bright or sunny intervals and isolated showers, wind NW, light, occasionally moderate, max temp 18°C (64°F).' Although the wedding was neither an official public holiday nor a State occasion, just 'a family affair', part of that family was royal, and the national newspapers and television companies had striven for weeks to promote speculation, interest and excitement concerning the main participants and the event. They succeeded, despite themselves. For the occasion itself was truly spectacular, a superbly staged, climactic episode in the continuing saga of a real Dynasty, a Dynasty distinguished by every attribute of rank and riches, but whose actual personalities and lifestyles, though much imagined, were largely unknown, and thus embodied fantasy.

Some fantasies might be malign, and complex security arrangements had been made to forestall and meet any terrorist threat. Westminster Abbey was virtually closed to the public a week before the wedding, when it was thoroughly searched and scoured by sniffer dogs trained to detect explosives. Concurrently, every nook was cleaned, cumbrous television equipment, scaffolding and lights installed, lengths of blue carpet laid, and palatial displays of flowers set in place. Two thousand policemen and women were on duty that day, many armed: some mingling with the crowds, some on rooftops, some riding with the carriages disguised as footmen, some on standy-by. Every house along the wedding route had been checked and checked again, pillar-boxes sealed, and remote-controlled video cameras set up to record their own peculiar aspects of the day.

Better pictures in every way would be garnered by the TV cameras, beginning at 6.15am, beaming them live to 500 million watchers of the box around the globe. Forty cameras, connected by 35 miles of cable, were employed by the BBC; ITV used 54. The listeners of BBC and commercial radio were boosted by the World Service to some 100 million; and dozens of foreign broadcasting companies ensured a worldwide audience of almost 750 million, the biggest since the World Cup in Mexico earlier in the year.

Some came to see for themselves, the vanguard settling on the pavements outside the Abbey on Monday morning, provided with sleeping-bags, plastic loungers, deck chairs, patriotic hats and balloons, supplies of food and drink, anoraks and umbrellas. Offices and pubs had rented window space, and whole floors to the more opulent for as much as £1,000 a day. In the streets where parking restrictions began at 6.0am on the Wednesday, the sellers of souvenir programmes, flags, drinks, periscopes, and party hats reaped a holiday harvest from the prodigal crowds, passing the sunny early morning hours until the passing show by tuning in to portable TV sets and radios and every glad distraction (even when handbags were searched) as the pavements shrank about them. The roads were swept; police numbers increased; first-aid men assembled; marching soldiers, sailors and airmen came to a halt along the ceremonial route, facing each other (the police faced the crowds across the barriers); 1,600

The Glass Coach, in which Sarah Ferguson rode with her father from Clarence House to the Abbey, was built in 1910. It was last used by the Princess of Wales at her wedding in 1981, and at the wedding of the Queen Mother in 1923. The Coach first appeared at the Coronation in 1911 of Prince Andrew's great-grandparents, King George V and Queen Mary. In recent years special interior lighting was added so that the public could have a good view of the bride. Two bay horses, Brown Owl and Goshawk, drew the Coach, driven by royal coachman, Cecil Nelson. One of the footmen, Andrew McGill, aged 23, from Liverpool, and unemployed two years ago, answered an advertisement in a Jobcentre – 'Footman in household required; district, London; possibility of travel.'

The Marriage of
HRH The Prince Andrew & Miss Sarah Ferguson
Westminster Abbey, 23 July 1986

ORDER OF SERVICE

Fanfare

During the Procession of the Bride there shall be played
Imperial March ... Edward Elgar

Fanfare

Then all shall join in singing the Hymn

Praise to the Lord, the Almighty, the King of Creation

THE FORM OF SOLEMNIZATION OF MATRIMONY
Shall be conducted by THE DEAN OF WESTMINSTER *and* THE ARCHBISHOP OF CANTERBURY. *After the Archbishop has blessed the Couple, all shall be seated and the Choir shall sing a Motet*
We wait for thy loving kindness, O God
 ... William McKie

Then shall follow
THE LESSON
read by
HIS ROYAL HIGHNESS
THE PRINCE OF WALES
Ephesians 3 : 14 to the end

Then all shall stand and join in singing the Hymn Lead us, heavenly Father, lead us

The hymn ended, the congregation shall kneel for

THE PRAYERS
said by the Precentor and Sacrist
THE LORD'S PRAYER and the RESPONSES

Then THE CARDINAL ARCHBISHOP of WESTMINSTER *shall say*
Almighty God, giver of life and love, bless ANDREW and SARAH, whom thou hast now joined in Christian marriage. Grant them wisdom and devotion in their life together, that each may be to the other a strength in need, a comfort in sorrow, and a companion in joy. So unite their wills in thy will, and their spirits in thy Spirit, that they live and grow together in love and peace all the days of their life; through Jesus Christ our Lord. *Amen*

THE MODERATOR OF THE GENERAL ASSEMBLY OF THE CHURCH OF SCOTLAND
shall say
Almighty God, our heavenly Father, who hast given marriage to be a source of blessing to mankind, we thank thee for the joys of family life. May we know thy presence and peace in our homes; fill them with thy love, and use them for thy glory; through Jesus Christ our Lord. *Amen*

THE MODERATOR OF THE FREE CHURCH FEDERAL COUNCIL
shall say
O merciful Lord, and heavenly Father, by whose gracious gift mankind is increased: We beseech thee, assist with thy blessing these two persons, that they may both be fruitful in procreation of children, and also live together so long in godly love and honesty, that they may see their children christianly and virtuously brought up, to thy praise and honour; through Jesus Christ our Lord. *Amen*

THE CHAPLAIN OF THE FLEET *shall say the Prayer of Sir Francis Drake*
O Lord God, when thou givest to thy servants to endeavour any great matter, grant us also to know that it is not the beginning, but the continuing of the same until it be thoroughly finished, which yieldeth the true glory; through him, who for the finishing of thy work laid down his life: our Saviour, Jesus Christ. *Amen*

THE ARCHBISHOP OF YORK *shall say*
Almighty God, Father of all mercies and giver of all grace, we ask thy blessing on the members of the Royal Family as they fulfil their service among us; that both by their word and example our nation and commonwealth may be strengthened in love of righteousness and freedom, and preserved in unity and peace; through Jesus Christ our Lord. *Amen*

and continue with
THE BLESSING OF THE COUPLE
Almighty God, the Father of our Lord Jesus Christ, pour upon you the riches of his grace, sanctify and bless you, that ye may please him both in body and soul, and live together in holy love unto your lives' end. *Amen*

The Congregation shall remain kneeling while the Choir sings
THE ANTHEM
Set me as a seal upon thine heart
 ... William Walton

The Congregation standing, all shall sing the Hymn
Come down, O Love divine

All shall kneel, and
THE ARCHBISHOP OF CANTERBURY
shall pronounce
THE BLESSING

God the Holy Trinity make you strong in faith and love, defend you on every side, and guide you in truth and peace; and the blessing of God Almighty, the Father, the Son, and the Holy Spirit, be among you and remain with you always.

After a sung Amen and Fanfare, all shall stand to sing

THE NATIONAL ANTHEM

During the Signing of the Register, then two motets shall be sung
Laudate Dominum ... W. A. Mozart
Exultate, Jubilate ... W. A. Mozart

After the Signing of the Registers a Fanfare shall be sounded and there shall be played
The Triumphal March from Caractacus
 ... Edward Elgar
Crown Imperial
 ... William Walton

servicemen would stand at kerbside attention for over two hours.

At 8.0am the news broke that the Queen had created her second son and future daughter-in-law Duke and Duchess of York – another chance for the crowds to renew the celebrations that had begun with singing, dancing and carousing in the Mall overnight. Overhead an occasional police helicopter clattered by; a silvered airship bearing the words 'Good Luck' hove into view; and from 8.30, when there was a slight shower, the flag-bedecked, bannered and now thronging roads of central London, 92 in all, were cordoned off and closed to traffic. Myriads of voices replaced the usual mechanical rumpus of the streets.

Most of the talk was of what was in the papers and what had been on television the night before. Between 7 and 8pm, BBC TV and ITV had shown differently edited versions of the same material, that pictured the Prince and Sarah at work and play, being both conscientious and frolicsome, and contentedly dealing with the questions posed by Andrew Gardner and Sue Lawley during a lengthy interview in Prince Andrew's Palace sitting-room. They were much more relaxed and expressive than they had been in the engagement interview. Before it was recorded (on Monday, 14 July), they sang 'Happy Birthday' to Sue Lawley, 40 that day. Sarah had confessed that the weeks before the wedding had been 'a lot of hard work, and I do get very tired'. 'But,' she said, 'the novelty won't ever wear off. I love it;' Although she said she didn't have a temper – Andrew interposed that she wasn't *red-haired*, but *'Titian'*. 'Changes with the weather,' he said. 'A very interesting colour.' – she admitted: 'I am quite opinionated.' She was adamant she was quite happy with her own figure – 'I'm quite happy with myself.' She didn't diet, and had stopped reading what was written about her by the press. Of her wardrobe – 'Dress how *you* want to dress,' urged Andrew – she said: 'I'm not too hot on organising my clothes. Bit of a grind ... I'm not a great clothes-horse, but I'm getting quite patient.' She revealed she was not too keen on cooking, and intended to learn how to fly. 'I want to be able to sit down at dinner and discuss what he's done during the day. Flying is his life, and I want to be part of his life.' She added: 'I'm very proud of my boy.' Nobody mentioned love. But it was very evident that the couple adored each other, and rejoiced in each other's company.

They had spent the day before the wedding at Buckingham Palace, sorting out last-minute arrangements. That morning, the Queen held an investiture there, while the Duke of Edinburgh attended a reception at St James's Palace. That evening, Sarah was driven to Clarence House, the London home of the Queen Mother, while the Ferguson and Makim families drove up to London from Dummer, which had been taken over by the media circus, to stay overnight at the Belgravia Sheraton Hotel. The Princess of Wales, having attended a performance given by the Bolshoi Ballet at the Royal Opera House, called at Clarence House on her way home to Kensington Palace.

Sarah can hardly have slept that night, beset with all sorts of imaginings about the wedding day, and possibly kept awake by the riotous sounds of carnival in the Mall. Drivers hooted their horns, and blared music from car radios and cassettes until after midnight. But at last the bride and the intemperate revellers were able to get some sleep.

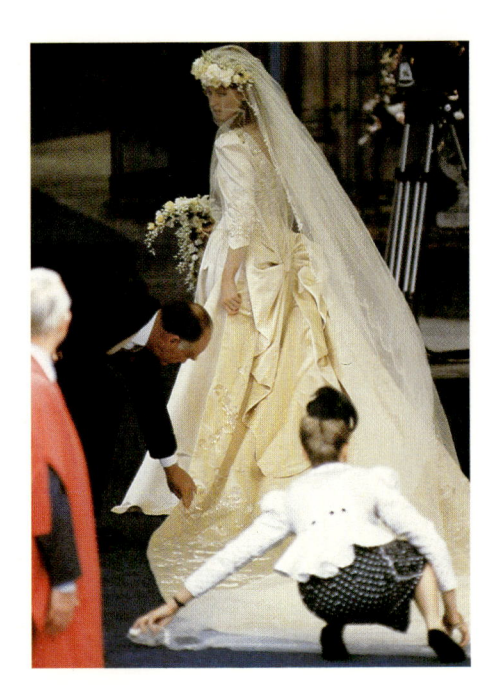

She woke at dawn. A cup of coffee, and then began the protracted preparations for her appearance before the eyes of millions. Now and then she glanced at television reports and glimpsed the cold and sleepy people stirring in the Mall. Her hair was washed and carefully styled; her hands manicured and her make-up applied. Maybe there was time for something to eat. Then Lindka Cierach began assisting her with the wedding dress and the train. Lastly, the veil with its band of cream and yellow flowers was securely pinned in place.

Meanwhile, people came to admire, to chat, to help a little and cheer the bride: her mother, stepmother, the Queen Mother, and Sarah's sister, Jane. Perhaps the bridegroom telephoned to exchange a joke to share and quell any personal apprehensions. In due course, the pages and bridesmaids arrived, followed by Major Ronald Ferguson. He waited below, until it was time for his daughter to descend the stairs.

At Westminster Abbey, at 10am, the Great West Door was opened to admit the first of the wedding guests, 1,800 of them, crowding into the brilliant nave, lit by the magnificent Waterford crystal chandeliers, and perfumed by the thousands of flowers adorning the walls, the choir screen and altar in glorious profusion. One hundred ushers were at hand to direct them to their seats, and hand out service sheets. In addition, the Abbey staff of about two hundred, including bell-ringers and honorary stewards, went about their specific tasks for that day, supervised by Reg Pullen, the Abbey's Receiver General, who had been involved in the arrangements for four royal weddings, beginning with that of the Queen. The choir – 12 men (all members of Equity) and 22 boys – having been ousted from their usual seats below, crammed themselves onto the organ loft with the orchestra and trumpeters of the Royal Marines.

By half-past ten, the nave was nearly full; the women's outfits a focus of special attention, as well as the occasional famous face: Michael Caine, Elton John, David Frost, Billy Connolly, Anthony Andrews, Jackie Stewart, were there with their wives. Then, as a final inspection of the entire wedding route was carried out on horseback by the Chief of Staff of the London District and his deputies, other notable persons appeared in the nave, passing under the organ loft into the choir: diplomats, politicians and heads of state. King Constantine of the Hellenes and his family arrived as the plastic sheets covering the main aisle were removed to reveal blue carpeting. Rich Persian carpets covered the floor of the sanctuary itself.

At 10.42 Mrs Thatcher and her husband joined the congregation, followed at 10.45 (as the Queen Mother was leaving Clarence House by car for Buckingham Palace) by Mr and Mrs Hector Barrantes, who joined the members of the Ferguson family seated on the north side of the sanctuary – including Sarah's uncle, Bryan Fitzherbert Wright (her mother's only brother), an ex-major in the Blues and Royals and now a family butler. Last of the principal guests to arrive was Mrs Nancy Reagan, wife of the President of the United States. The Abbey organist and choir master, Simon Preston, began to play. 'The Trumpet Tune and Air' by Henry Purcell.

The crush of people outside Clarence House in Stable Yard Road were the first to see how the bridesmaids and pages were dressed, as they left by car for the Abbey. Five minutes later, the first of the processions to leave Buckingham Palace emerged. Four black, stately limousines bore the royal families of the Gloucesters, the Kents and the Ogilvys through the cheering crowds and into the Mall. Then the Queen's Carriage Procession, accompanied by a Sovereign's Escort of the Household Cavalry, left the

The wedding dress, designed by Lindka Cierach, was made of rich ivory silk duchess satin. The silk for the dress was manufactured at Britain's only silk farm, near Sherborne in Dorset, where about 2,000 silk-worms, fed on mulberry leaves, spun the cocoons from which the silver threads were taken. The fitted boned bodice had a dropped waist coming into a point at the front and a lower 'V' at the back. The sleeves were full and square, coming into a simple pearl-edged point below the elbow, and the underskirt was finished with a silk scalloped lace flounce. The train flowed from beneath a fan-shaped bow; it was 17½ft long. The beadwork on the dress was based on Sarah's Coat of Arms and portrayed thistles, bees, and an 'S' for Sarah. These were interwoven with anchors, waves and hearts on the train, rising in scale at the bottom, where a heraldic 'A' led into a double 'S'. The veil was made of pure silk bobinet beaded with sequins and scattered with embroidered hearts along the edge, punctured with guipure lace.

The bride's satin shoes were designed by Manolo Blahnik, and beaded with bees and ribbons in pearl and diamonds. Sarah's hair on the wedding day was styled by Denise McAdam of Michaeljohn, and she was made up by Teresa Fairminer, a freelance make-up artist. Her head-dress was made up of lilies of the valley, lily petals, and small cream roses and gardenias.

She wore a necklace of cultured pearls intertwined with 18 carat gold and diamond rondels, with a diamond and pearl pendent.

The bouquet contained lilies of the valley, gardenias, lilies, veronica, and myrtle from a sprig grown from Queen Victoria's wedding bouquet.

The bride's bouquet was designed by Jane Packer, aged 26, and made up by a team of girls, headed by Mrs Doris Wellham, of the City florists, Longmans. Two bouquets were used on the wedding day, the first being presented at Clarence House at 8.0am; the other was delivered to the Palace three hours later and used at the formal picture session there. The floral displays in the Abbey, involving more than 20,000 blooms, were arranged by 40 volunteers from the National Association of Flower Arranging Societies. It took them two days.

The bridesmaids' dresses were made in soft peach taffeta silk, trimmed with an ecru and peach cotton lace. The fitted bodices had a V-shaped panel, back and front, beaded with bows and bugles. The lace on the dresses featured thistles, bees and bows, in a peach thread with an ecru cord outline, all made and designed in Nottingham. The bridesmaids wore half-circlets of peach roses, lilies of the valley and freesias on their heads, and carried hoops bound with peach satin ribbon and bunches of peach roses, lilies of the valley, and freesias.

Two of the pages, Peter Phillips and Andrew Ferguson, wore 18th century midshipmen's full dress uniforms, designed and made by Gieves and Hawkes, the Savile Row tailors. Victorian sailor suits were worn by Prince William and Seamus Makim.

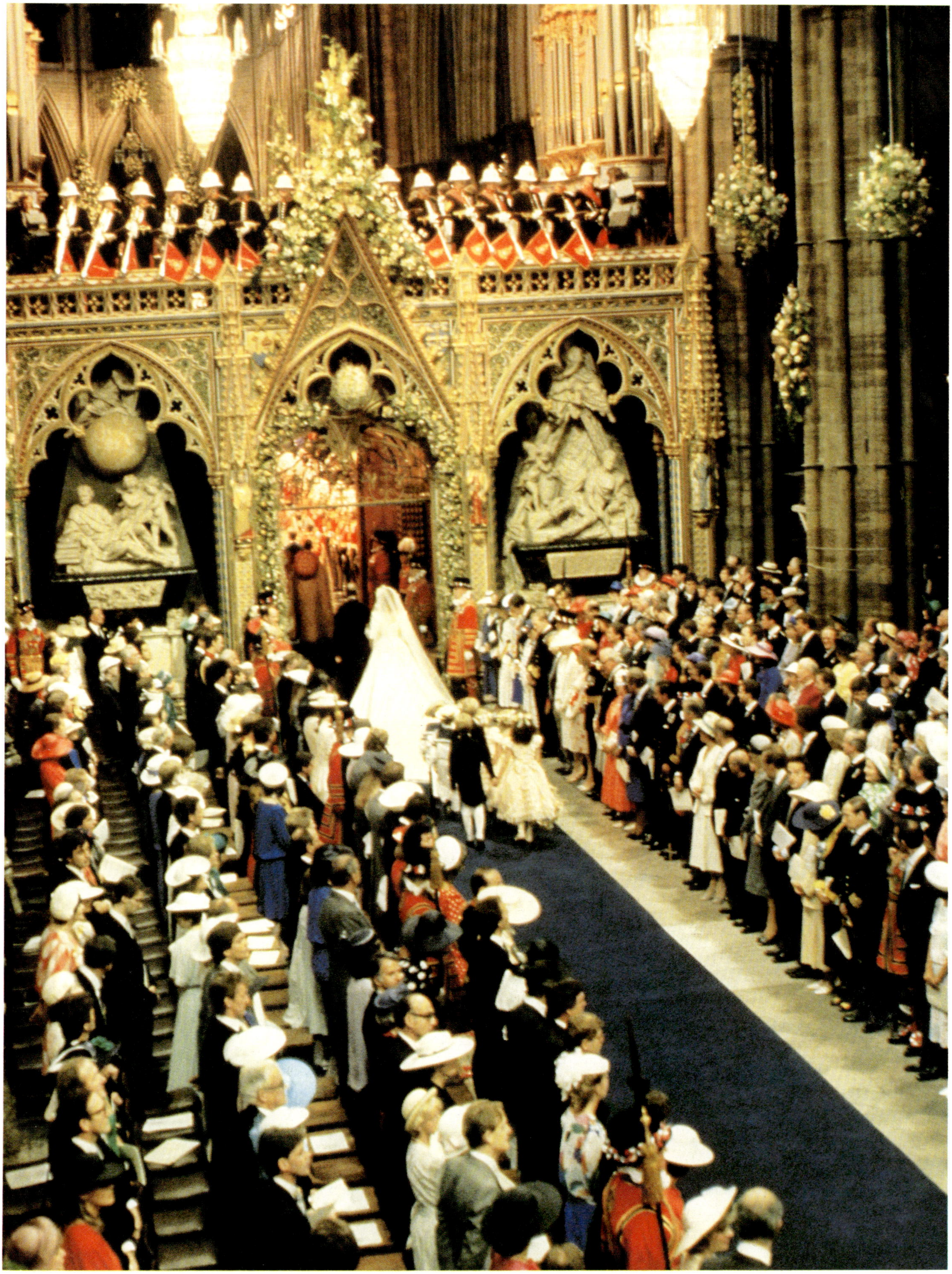

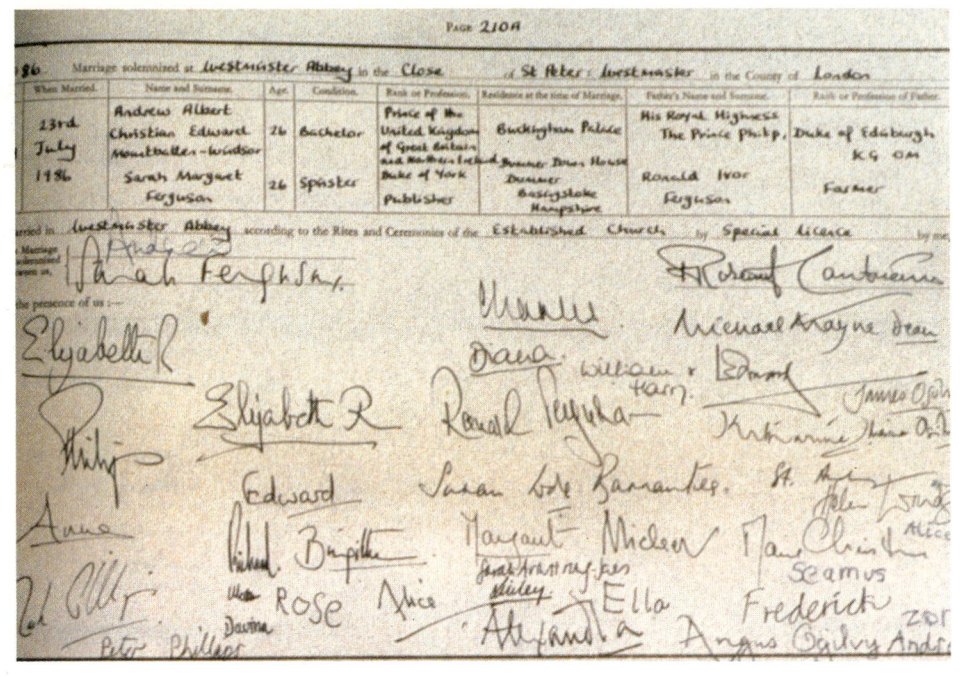

The Queen's Procession as it left the Abbey was led by two Gentlemen Ushers (Air Chief Marshall Sir Neville Stack and Capt Michael Barrow, RN); then came the Earl of Airlie, with the Duke of Northumberland. Following the Queen and Major Ferguson were the Duke of Edinburgh and Mrs Hector Barrantes; and the Earl of Dalhousie, Lord Chamberlain to the Queen Mother. With her were the Prince and Princess of Wales; then came Princess Margaret, flanked by her two children; and the three children of the Duke and Duchess of Gloucester, who walked with their mother, Princess Alice, Duchess of Gloucester. The two children of the Duke and Duchess of Kent preceded their parents, as did the two young children of Prince and Princess Michael of Kent, and the son and daughter of Princess Alexandra and the Hon Angus Ogilvy. Major Ferguson's morning dress, which he wore at both his previous marriages, was originally worn by his father, at *his* wedding in 1927.

Palace. She and the Duke of Edinburgh, in a Semi-State Landau, were followed by four other carriages containing the Queen Mother, Princess Margaret, Viscount Linley, Lady Sarah Armstrong-Jones; the Prince and Princess of Wales; Princess Anne, Capt Mark Philips and the Earl of Westmorland; and chief members of the Royal Household. As the Queen's landau proceeded on its way, the military bands along the wedding route paused in their playing of popular tunes to mark her progress with one verse of the National Anthem.

The last procession to leave the Palace was that of the Bridegroom. He and Prince Edward were conveyed in the 1902 State Landau. Prince Andrew wore the ceremonial day dress of a Royal Naval Lieutenant. The medals on his uniform were the South Atlantic Campaign Medal and the Jubilee Medal; the Royal Victorian Order was around his neck. His brother was in the No. 1 dress uniform of the Royal Marines (full blues and a Sam Brown belt and brown gloves), in which he is an acting Lieutenant. The Guard of Honour gave the two Princes a royal salute, and the band played the first six bars of the National Anthem.

The Queen's Carriage Procession reached the Abbey at 11.10am, as the Bridegroom's drove down the Mall. At the Great West Door, the Queen and the Duke of Edinburgh were received by the Dean and Chapter of Westminster before they made their way up the aisle, preceded by two Gentleman Ushers; by 25 senior members of the Royal Family; by Queen Elizabeth the Queen Mother and her Lord Chamberlain; by the Lord Steward, and the Lord Chamberlain, the Earl of Airlie, aged 60, who had supervised all the ceremonial events connected with the wedding.

Sarah Ferguson left Clarence House with her father, Major Ferguson, in the Glass Coach at 11.15am, accompanied by a small escort of Life Guards – a special concession to Major Ferguson and his family's long association with them. A limousine trailed behind the Coach in case it broke down. The eager eyes of the crowd and of the millions of television viewers caught tantalizing glimpses of the wedding dress, the circlet of flowers and the veil that could not conceal her happiness, nor her red hair. Heaped in front of her was the train, as yet only partly visible. She gaily waved, showing none of the nervousness that she must have felt.

The bells of St Margaret's Church, Westminster, were pealing as Prince Andrew arrived at the Abbey. Outside it, seamen and senior ratings who had served with him lined the approach to the Great West Door. He was greeted by a humorous chorus from the crowd of 'The Grand Old Duke of York', and as he passed under the blue-and-white canvas awning, he grinned with pleasure to see his former shipmates. Once inside, the Chaplain of Westminster Abbey led him and Prince Edward to the Chapel of St Edmund, to await the arrival of the bride.

The Glass Coach reached the Abbey at 11.28am, exactly on time. Lindka Cierach and her assistant darted forward to straighten the creases of the bridal gown and spread out the bride's voluminous train. Sarah had said, 'There will never be a dress to match it', and her words were amply realised. Every intricate detail had been so carefully planned and executed that the wedding dress was completely individual, a triumph for both wearer and designer. As the bride entered the Abbey, on the arm of her father, the trumpeters of the Royal Marines heralded her arrival.

After being greeted by the new Dean, she moved forward around the Tomb of the Unknown Warrior and paused while the bridal procession formed. The pages and bridesmaids, who had been waiting for half an hour, stopped their excited chattering. Holding hands, the pages and bridesmaids, with the smallest in front – Prince William and Laura Fellowes – followed the bride up the nave, careful not to step on her train. The organ played the Imperial March by Elgar.

Prince Andrew, who had taken his place with Prince Edward at the foot of the Sacrarium steps, looked to his left, beaming with delight as his bride appeared through the choir screen. At the steps she hesitated, then moved cautiously up them towards the altar, stopping in front of the two kneelers, with her father on her left and Prince Andrew on her right. She turned and gave her bouquet to the eldest bridesmaid, Lady Rosanagh. Programmes containing the Order of Service were now opened – the marriage ceremony began.

Another fanfare led into the opening hymn. The Very Reverend Michael Mayne, the Dean of Westminster, introduced the service, beginning 'Dearly beloved, we are gathered here in the sight of God...' Prince Andrew stood throughout at attention, with his left hand on his sword; Sarah clasped her hands in front of her. Then the Archbishop of Canterbury, Dr Robert Runcie, took the couple through their vows. Both spoke firmly and clearly. As each said, 'I will', a cheer arose from the crowds outside and could be heard within the Abbey. The couple had decided to follow the liturgy of the 1662 Book of Common Prayer. Sarah had chosen to 'obey', saying so, twice, because – 'In a dilemma there will always have to be someone who makes the final decision. I shall leave that decision to my husband.'

When the Archbishop asked, 'Who giveth this woman to be married to this man?' Major Ferguson very deliberately presented his daughter's left hand to Dr Runcie, who in turn placed it under Prince Andrew's right hand. So determined was the bridegroom not to make a mistake in repeat-

The five-tiered wedding cake was made in the kitchens of the Royal Naval Supply School at HMS *Raleigh*, Torpoint in Cornwall, by CPO Trevor Spicer, aged 39; Sgt Alan Starling, 30, of the Royal Marines; and 20-year-old Wren Steward Mandy Platt. Using non-toxic children's paint, Wren Platt painted the motifs on the cake. It weighed 240lbs, was 5' 6" high and contained 15 ingredients, with lashings of rum, brandy and port. Completed a week before the wedding, the cake and an exact duplicate (in case of accidents) were brought in sections to London, packed in wooden crates. The motifs on the bottom tier showed places like the couple's homes and the Abbey; the next bore the crests of ships and squadrons, in which Prince Andrew had served; the middle tier had pictures of Sarah's choice (a polo player, Pegasus, and Van Gogh's *Sunflowers*); the next, Prince Andrew's armorial bearings; and the top tier bore the monogram of an entwined A and S.

ing his vows that his eyes never left the service sheet on the kneeler before him. Sarah in her turn, despite her device for remembering his christian names (Andrew plus ACE), stumbled, repeating 'Christian' twice. As she promised 'to obey' she looked at him; and as she said, 'I give thee my troth,' she smiled.

Prince Edward now produced the wedding ring. When Prince Andrew put the ring on the fourth finger of Sarah's left hand, he failed to push it quite far enough, and eventually she had to tug it into place herself. Unexpectedly, she then gave the Prince a ring in exchange. They knelt, as the Archbishop said, 'Let us pray'. The congregation still stood as Dr Runcie blessed the couple, trusting that they would 'ever remain in perfect love and peace together.' Then, after joining together their right hands, he pronounced them man and wife. At that moment Sarah Ferguson became the Duchess of York.

The congregation seated themselves as a motet was sung. Prince Charles read the lesson, and everyone then stood to sing 'Lead us, heavenly Father, lead us' – a hymn often sung at Sarah's school and traditional at naval weddings. There was no sermon. The wedded couple advanced to the high altar as Prince Edward and Major Ferguson went to their seats and the kneelers were taken away.

The Precentor and Sacrist now led the congregation in prayer – the five prayers following the Lord's Prayer being read by leading churchmen,

The wedding ring, a plain band of gold, was made from the same nugget of Welsh gold from which the wedding rings of five other royal brides were crafted. They were: the Queen Mother, who married the then Duke of York – later George VI – in 1923, Queen Elizabeth II, Princess Margaret, Princess Anne and the Princess of Wales. The nugget, discovered before the First World War and kept by the Crown jewellers, Garrard, whose craftsmen have created all six royal wedding rings, came from the Clogau St David mine at Dolgellau.

Prince Andrew is the 14th Duke of York, a title created by Richard II for his uncle, Edmund of Langley, just over 600 years ago, in 1385. The second Duke was killed at Agincourt; the fifth, Richard, was one of the two young Princes murdered in the Tower of London. The Grand Old Duke of York, featured in the nursery rhyme, was Frederick, second son of George III, Commander-in-Chief of the British Army. Five of the Dukes, Edward IV, Henry VIII, James II, George V, and George VI, became king. The last four were second sons, like Prince Andrew, but his chances of being crowned are remote. After the birth of his nephews, the Princes William and Henry, he has fallen to fourth in the order of succession to the throne.

The official photographs of the royal wedding were taken by Albert Mackenzie Watson, aged 43, a fashion photographer. Born in Edinburgh, he is married with two sons, and now works in New York. He graduated at the Royal College of Art in London. Prince Andrew, an admirer of Watson's photographic skills, mainly on display in magazines like *Vogue*, invited him to lunch last year at Buckingham Palace to discuss his methods. Lord Snowdon said: 'His work is distinguished by impeccable lighting, great style and elegance.' Mr Watson said of the commission: 'I have to do everything I can to make it go smoothly. My only concern is the time aspect. When everyone comes through the door I shall need to be quite firm. I want it to look amazing.' The announcement of Mr Watson's appointment, a complete break with royal tradition, was made on 10 July, on the day that Sarah Ferguson opened an exhibition of Prince Andrew's photographs at the Royal Albert Hall. The pictures were mainly of snowy landscapes. Earlier, Mr Watson had said: 'I think he has real sympathy with landscapes. I told him last year he should do more and more of that.' Gene Nocon, Prince Andrew's photographic adviser, assisted Mr Watson at the formal picture session at the Palace, and took the informal, more personal photos for the bride and groom.

After the wedding, the couple will have an income of about £77,000 a year, not much for a Duke and Duchess, but a lot for a naval Lieutenant and his wife. To her salary of about £12,000, can be added his, about £14,000. He will also receive an increment of £30,000 to the £20,000 from the Civil List that is his on his marriage.

Overleaf the wedding group photographed by Albert Watson. Front row, seated, left to right: The Earl of Ulster, Lady Davina Windsor, Lady Rose Windsor, Andrew Ferguson, Lady Rosanagh Innes-Ker, Zara Phillips, Prince William of Wales, Laura Fellowes, Seamus Makim, Alice Ferguson, Peter Phillips, Lady Gabriella Windsor, Lord Frederick Windsor. Second row: Lady Sarah Armstrong-Jones, Princess Margaret, Princess Anne, Princess Diana holding Prince Henry, the Queen Mother, the Queen, the bride and groom, Major Ronald Ferguson, Prince Edward, Mrs Susan Barrantes, Lady Elmhirst, Mrs Jane Makim. Slightly behind them: the Hon. Mrs Doreen Wright, Major Bryan Wright, Alexander Makim. Third Row: Viscount Linley, Captain Mark Phillips, Marina Ogilvy, the Prince of Wales, Princess Alexandra, the Duke of Edinburgh, Princess Michael of Kent, Princess Alice, the Duchess of Gloucester, the Duchess of Kent, Lady Helen Windsor. Back row: James Ogilvy, Prince Michael of Kent, the Hon. Angus Ogilvy, the Duke of Gloucester, the Duke of Kent, and the Earl of St. Andrews.

83

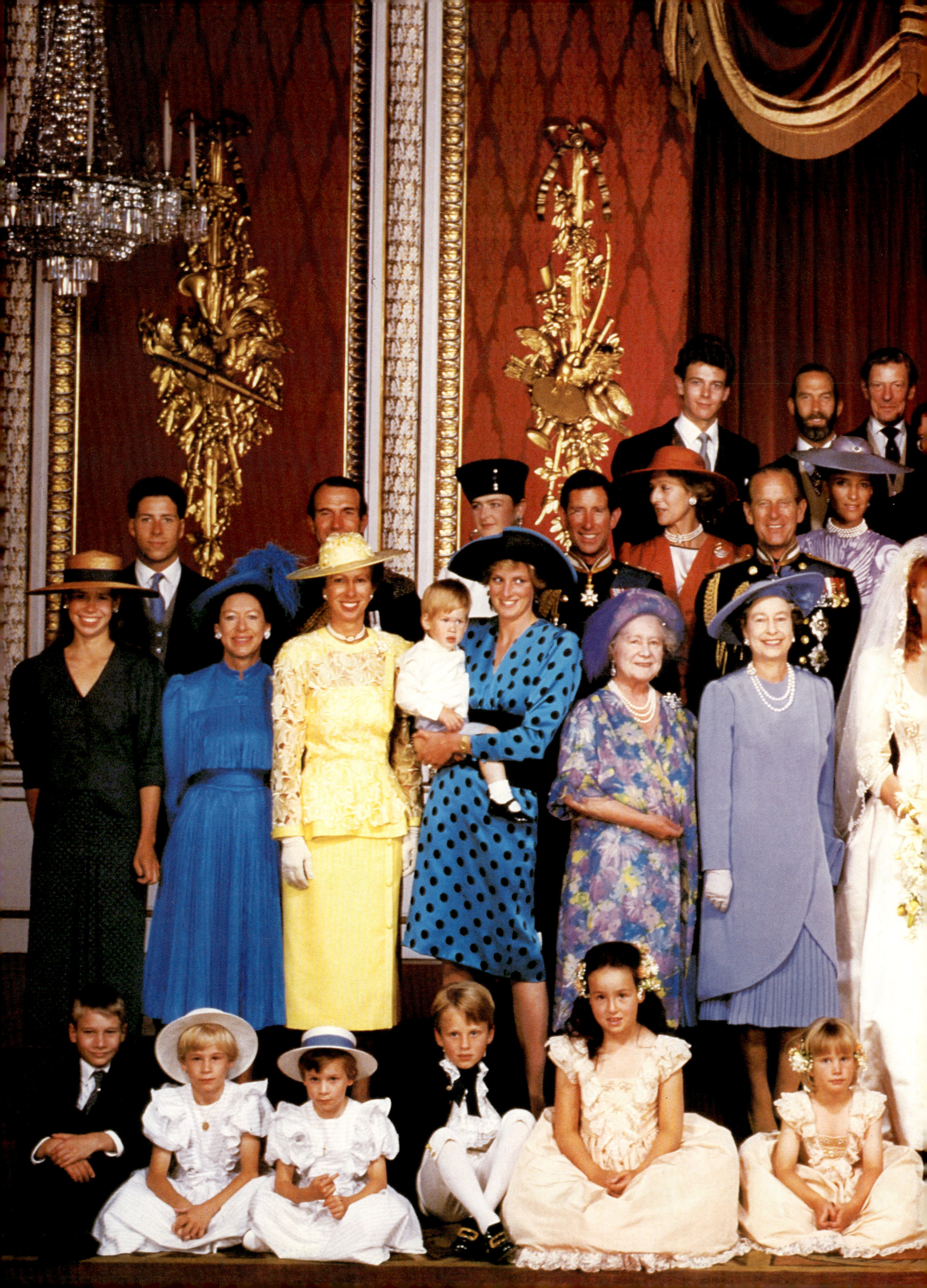

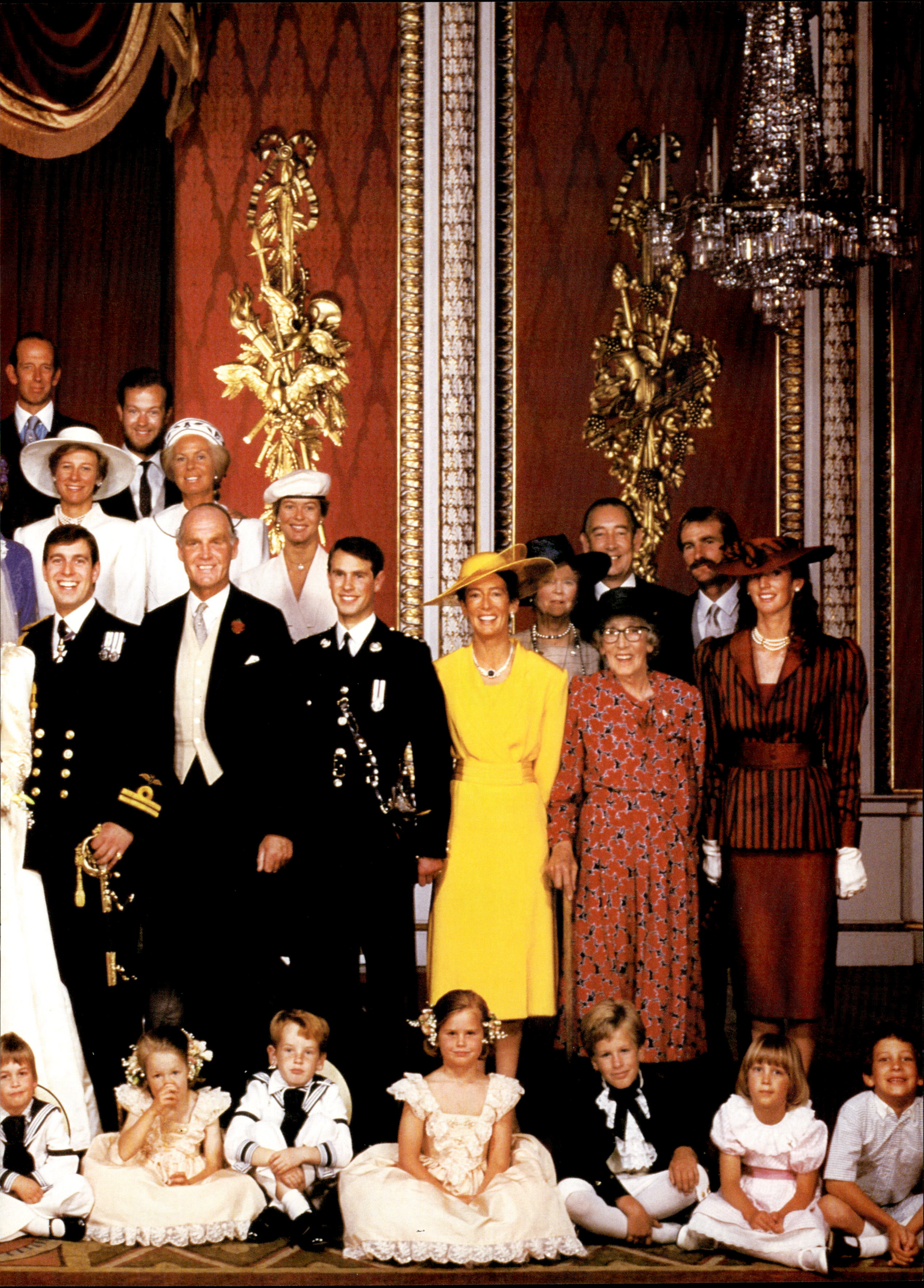

ending with the Archbishop of York. The Anthem followed, and everyone stood again for the concluding hymn, which preceded the final blessing (given by the Archbishop of Canterbury), the sung 'Amen', and the National Anthem.

It was now time for the signing of the registers, one for the Royal Family, and two for the Abbey. The bride and groom were led into the Chapel of St Edward the Confessor by Dr Runcie; the bride's bouquet was returned to her by Lady Rosanagh, who helped to rearrange the train with the assistance of Peter Phillips. The Queen and her husband followed their son and new daughter-in-law into the Chapel, preceding the Queen Mother, Prince Edward, Major Ferguson and Mrs Barrantes. The rest of the families' signatures would be acquired later at Buckingham Palace.

While the registers were being signed, two motets by Mozart were sung from the organ loft by Felicity Lott and Arleen Auger. The Princess of Wales was seen to be amused by Prince William's antics, chewing and playing with the cord of his hat. Throughout the service, the women of both families had kept a wary but kindly eye on their offspring seated on stools below the sanctuary steps. When Major Ferguson returned to his seat after the registers were signed, he turned to exchange several words with his wife, Susan.

The Clergy Procession formed and proceeded down the aisle. Hand-in-hand, the new Duke and Duchess of York returned to the Sanctuary, she with her veil thrown back and wearing a diamond tiara loaned by a family friend. As the 'Triumphal March' from *Caractacus* was played on the organ, they stepped towards the Queen: Sarah curtsied and Andrew bowed. Now they looked happy, and somewhat relieved that the formality of the service was over. They advanced down the aisle, between the Gentlemen at Arms and then the Yeoman of the Guard, smiling to left and right at friends and faces they recognised. They were followed by their eight small attendants and in due course by the Queen's Procession. Major Ferguson walked with the Queen, and Mrs Barrantes with the Duke of Edinburgh. As Prince Andrew reached the Tomb of the Unknown Warrior his naval cap was returned to him.

The Abbey's ten bells rang out, and would ring a full peal for over three hours, as the Prince and his bride emerged into the sunshine from the Great West Door, to the joyful acclamation of the crowd. It was nearly 12.30pm, the service having overrun by five minutes. The newly-weds waved, and hardly stopped waving until they reached Buckingham Palace. They travelled there in the 1902 State Landau, with a silver horse-shoe on the seat before them, a gift from the Royal Mews. Just before Admiralty Arch, someone in the crowd showered them with rice and confetti. At one point, Sarah gave a thumbs-up sign.

The bridesmaids and pages travelled in two open carriages, giggling and waving wildly at the crowds, exulting in their freedom from restraint. When they scrambled out of their carriages in the Grand Entrance of Buckingham Palace, Prince William dashed up to his uncle Andrew for a hug and a kiss and then demanded the same of Sarah. Not to be outdone, the other children followed suit.

The Palace staff had gathered in the quadrangle and applauded the return of the Royal party, welcoming them home. The guests attending the wedding breakfast entered the Palace through a side entrance, as the Mall was now a river of festive humanity. Lines of police eased the crowds for-

Sarah's going-away outfit a white flower-printed pure silk crêpe de Chine dress, was designed by Mrs Suzanne Schneider, who runs the West End dress manufacturers, Sujon. Her designs are sold at stores like Harvey Nichols.

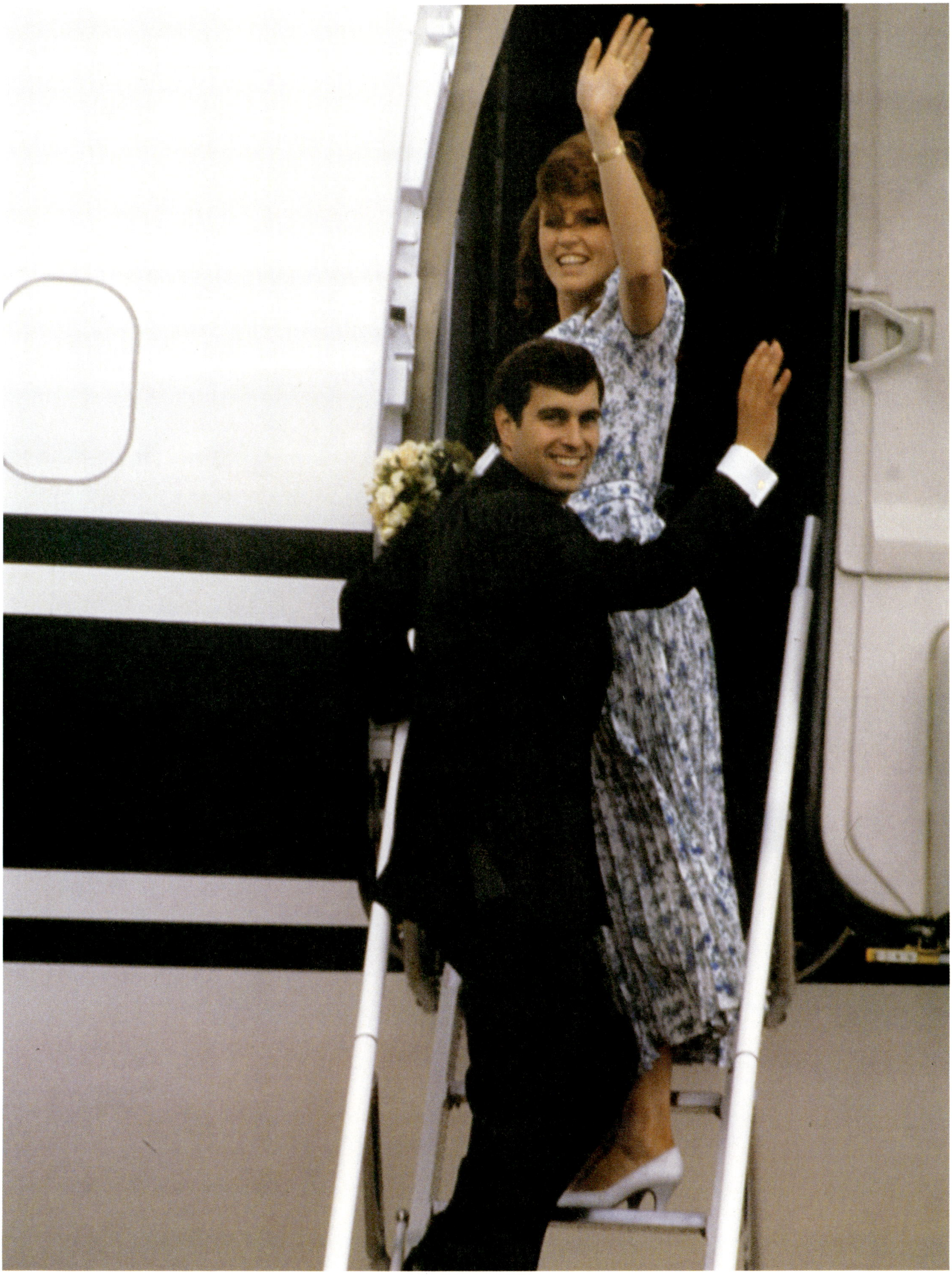

ward right up to the Palace railings. A brief shower at 1.00pm brought out some umbrellas, while inside the Palace the official wedding photographs were being taken by Albert Watson. He was so meticulous that the appearance on the balcony was delayed by half-an-hour. The crowds chanted, 'We want Fergie!' and shouted. 'A-N-D-Y. Andy!'

At 1.51pm, the bridal couple emerged at last from the Centre Room on the first floor, to the noisy delight of the waiting thousands below. Then the Queen led out the other members of the wedding party; the Princess of Wales carried her younger son, Harry, in her arms.

Sarah cupped her hand to her ear, seemingly unaware of what the crowd were now calling. So did Andrew. She turned to him, and without any further prompting he kissed her full on the lips. The rest of the family left the balcony, leaving the young couple alone, with their hands entwined.

After a brief four-minute appearance, the Duchess picked up her train and the couple went back inside. But they soon re-emerged to do an encore, to the final satisfaction of the crowd. This time Prince Andrew gathered up his wife's train and they disappeared from view. The crowd now began to disperse. But several hundred remained to hail the couple when they left on their honeymoon.

The wedding breakfast, held in the Ball Supper Room, was attended by 140 of the closest friends and relatives of the Duke and Duchess of York. They enjoyed a three-course luncheon: diced lobster decorated with prawns, egg and tomato; roast best end of lamb and spinach souffle with mushrooms; and strawberries and cream. Three fine wines were served, and as the guests enjoyed the meal, the band of the Irish Guards played a medley of popular music, including 'Me and My Girl' and 'We've Only Just Begun'. The wedding cake was cut by Prince Andrew, using his ceremonial sword.

The departure of the honeymoon couple was delayed – partly because of a short shower – and the wedding guests waited in the Grand Entrance of the Palace for twenty minutes. Meanwhile, a giant teddy bear provided by Prince Edward, was tied to the front seat of an open carriage, and a homemade satellite dish, bearing the legend 'Phone Home', was attached to the back. A bow-tie of pink and blue ribbons adorned the teddy bear and flags and ribbons festooned the carriage. At the rear, an 'L' plate dangled beside a horseshoe.

As the carriage set off, showered in confetti, the Queen was seen to run and pull Prince William away from the wheels. The guests went back inside laughing and joking, Prince Charles giving Harry a piggy-back.

At 4.35, the newly-weds reached their destination, the grounds of the Royal Hospital, Chelsea. There, a red Wessex helicopter was waiting to whisk them to Heathrow Airport. They said goodbye to the Lord Chamberlain, the Earl of Airlie, and Sarah gave him a kiss. At 4.41pm, the helicopter's blades began to turn, and it rose slowly into the air. It flew up river, heading westwards to Heathrow. Before long the Duke and Duchess of York were boarding the newest aircraft of the Queen's Flight, its airbrakes blazoned with the words, 'Just Married'.

The honeymooners were off to the Azores, to join the Royal Yacht *Britannia* for a cruise around the islands. The wedding had been the most public of family affairs – 'The best day of my life,' said Sarah. Now it was time for private happiness, a time to forge the bonds of a marriage that would last a lifetime.

ILLUSTRATION ACKNOWLEDGEMENTS

The author and publishers are especially grateful to Major Ronald and Mrs Susan Ferguson for permission to reproduce photographs from the family albums:

front endpapers (left), 42, 43, 44, 45, 46, 47, 48, 49, 50 (top & below right), 51, 52, 53 (left).

Other photographs are reproduced by kind permission of the following:

Godfrey Argent 24 (top); *Camera Press* 20 (below), 21 (right), 22 (right), 29, 30 (top right), 41 (below left), 55 (left); Cecil Beaton 20 (top); Leonard Bourne 37 (left); Bryn Colton 36 (top), 53 (right); Terence Donovan frontispiece, 5 (below), 6, 17, 41 (below left); Glen Harvey 38 (below right); Phil Rudge 40; John Scott 25 (below), 28 (below); Ian Swift 8; *J Allan Cash* 14; *Central Independent Television* 62 (below); *Bill Cooper* 64 (top); *Anthony Grant* 43 (below), 48 (Dummer Down Farm), 64 (below), 57 (below right); *Anwar Hussein* 67 (top); *Illustrated London News* 25 (top); *London News Service* 55 (below); *News International* 11; *Pacemaker Press International* 67 (right); *Press Association* 65 (top left & below right); *Rex Features* 9, 13 (top left & below), 21 (top left), 23 (top left and right & below right), 30 (top left & below), 31 (below), 32 (below), 36 (below), 37 (right), 38 (top right), 39 (top right & top left), 50 (below left) 59, 60 (below), 61, 62 (top right); *Syndication International* front endpapers (right), and back endpapers 1, 3, 13 (right), 15, 21 (below left), 23 (below left), 24 (below), 26 (top & below), 27 (top & below), 28 (top), 31 (top), 32 (top), 33, 34, 35, 38 (left), 39 (below), 41 (top left, top right, centre & below right), 54, 55 (top), 56 (top & below), 57 (top & below left), 58, 60 (top), 62 (top left), 63, 65 (top right & below left), 66, 67 (below); *Weidenfeld & Nicolson Archive* 5 (top), 57 (below right).

The photographs between pages 70 and 92 are reproduced courtesy of Camera press/Albert Watson, Anwar Hussein, the Press Association, Rex Features and Syndication International.

Sarah Ferguson's genealogical table (page 4) is based on research by Debrett's Peerage and Baronetage.

The front jacket illustration is courtesy of Syndication International.

Book design by Simon Bell and Joy FitzSimmons

Jacket design by Anita Turpin